Fresh From The Brewer

Fresh From The Brewer

Sips Of Wisdom From The
Carpenter's Cup
Volume II

Troy Brewer

x

Aventine Press

Published by Aventine Press
1023 4th Ave #204
San Diego CA, 92101
www.aventinepress.com

ISBN: 1-59330-441-2

Printed in the United States of America

\Brew·er\, n.

(1) One who brews; one whose occupation is to prepare malt liquors or hot beverages such as coffee. Source: Webster's Revised Unabridged Dictionary

(2) One that stirs things up or causes trouble. In action to be imminent; impending: "storms brewing on every frontier."

(3) The name of the trouble-making caffeinated coffee drinker that authored this book.

Sip carefully and enjoy!

For John

I dedicate this book to my good friend and brother In Christ, John Ledbetter.

I thank God for the testimony you have and for the victory you live. The Lord you love so much promises that your best days are not behind you. I can't wait to see what good things He has for you and your boys.

When I see you, I see Jesus. Thank you for being His friend and for being mine.

Table of Contents

INTRODUCTION

I have never been famous for drinking only one cup of anything. Moderation has typically been a malfunction for me so it is only right, that there should be an addition to the first Fresh from the Brewer.

Volume 2 is just like the first in that it is a collection of this last year's newspaper columns, but 2005 was a very different year. I would say that the difference in the two years and in the two books is a lot like the difference between two cups of coffee from two separate nations.

They are both the same product, both of them what you thought they would be but somehow distinctly unique and different.

For me 2005 was an extremely different year than 2004 and so was the flavor and attitude of my columns.

Increase and Expansion

We saw our first marks of success in branching out into four additional papers and received for the first time real "hate mail." I was so excited!

It was the first confirmation that I had a regular audience of readers that were not Christian. I had prayed and hoped that would happen.

I should have prayed though that my influence would win some over, but for the time I was happy that I was being read. I just had to trust the Lord that if I did my job in "brewing," He would do His job in getting folks to drink.

You can lead a horse to the coffee cup but you can't guarantee he is going to like it.

On the other hand, I began receiving cards and letters from people saying that they cut out and save my columns. One lady said she copied them and handed them out at her factory as a witnessing tool.

How cool is that!

The Disastrous Year In Review

2005 was a hard year full of national disasters and personal challenges.

The famous hurricane season was the most active on record. Twenty-seven named tropical storms with fourteen of them becoming hurricanes. Seven of the fourteen hurricanes became major hurricanes of category three or higher and five of those hit the United States.

My wife Leanna and I found ourselves in the middle of the Gulf of Mexico at the same time as hurricane Wilma. That was interesting.

For those of us in the disaster relief business, we had never seen the need so great. Open Door Ministries gave away right at a million pounds of food and possibly several million pounds of goods in those twelve months alone. It was a record breaking year in many respects.

Just two weeks after Katrina my outreach Pastor, Andy Daly, loaded up our outreach truck and we went to Baton Rouge with food, bedding and clothing.

We saw a lot of this year's disaster first hand and I think the seriousness of it all affected my columns in a significant way.

Overcoming Personal Loss

Personally, the Brewer's lost a house that was being built for us and a food warehouse for which we had already signed the paperwork and plans were underway for the move. It was a year of dealing with huge disappointment and learning to maintain an overcoming vision anyway.

The greatest loss we suffered was that of our very good friend and my personal secretary, Paula Ledbetter. Paula died suddenly in her sleep while I was in Central America on a mission trip. She was only 37 years old.

The neat thing about our church is that we are really not like a church, we are more like a family and the loss of Paula is greater than I can calculate. Paula's Tribute is one of these chapters and let me mention that seventeen people gave their hearts to the Lord at Paula's sendoff.

So you might notice a common theme throughout this year's **FRESH FROM THE BREWER**. You will notice a lot of writing on overcoming hardship and seeing victory in adversity.

There is a theme of being thankful when it's not easy and being real when other people can't be.

I have never been a morning person yet my best cups of coffee are when it's early and cold and no fun to be up at that hour. Hopefully, just like that, some of my best writing has been done in difficult hours.

The Lord's strength really is made perfect in our weakness so now you will understand why this year's cup is much stronger than last year's.

I tell you though, I managed to keep my wonderful sense of humor and the Lord anointed me for a whole new level of sarcasm. 2005 was the year I learned to "rant" in eloquent written tirades, which cracked me up, while I delivered cheap shots to the devil below the belt.

So while this collection may be more like a double shot of written espresso instead of a mild breakfast blend, I encourage you to go ahead and sip. There is always something a little bit sweet in every article.

Blessings and Peace on you and may you always drink from the Carpenter's cup. May it be warmth to your bones and refreshing to your soul, even when it's stronger than you would prefer it to be.

Enjoy

Troy A. Brewer
Joshua, Texas

Fresh From The Brewer

Volume II

AND NOW SERIOUISLY FOLKS

A big part of being able to deal with the day we live in, is knowing what and what not, to take seriously. This is a real challenge for all of us. After all, these are the days when Kinky Friedman is running for Texas Governor.

I pay the exuberant price of Texas Monthly magazine and put up with page after page of their ridiculous commercials just so I can turn to the back and read what brother Kinky has to say. He is by far my favorite fictional writer and to me the funniest in print, but I just can't see me voting for a guy that wears a dress under his cowboy hat.

A few months ago when the limp wristed writers of Texas Monthly turned their liberal claws onto the righteous of Johnson county, I finally had enough. The story was about Pastor Gloria Gillaspie of Burleson and her daughter's city counsel fight to keep sexually oriented businesses out of our fair city. Instead of them being portrayed as the heroes they are, they were falsely represented as "hoity-toity, do-gooders" that stand in the way of progress.

In so doing, Texas Monthly jumped in the same bed as a lot of other news groups and onto my "ugly" list. I would ask, "Is this Texas Monthly or Manhattan Monthly?" Sometimes it's hard to tell, but reading between the lines you will come to some quick conclusions.

If you build a life changing ministry from the ground up that helps and changes families for generations, very few will give a rip. But should you dare to stand against a pervert that sells perverse paraphernalia, you bring the thunder down on you. Go figure.

I tip my hat, (and I am not wearing a dress under mine) to those very few people who can stand the heat and stay in the kitchen for the rest of us. Contrary to what 20/20 or any other national news organization has to say, we do not want Johnson County to look like Harry Hines in Dallas. Should anybody want to move to the paradise of Shreveport we will be happy to send you a map.

I said all of that so that I could give a great big "Thank You" to Pastor Gillaspie and to her daughter Richelle Smithee. I appreciate the fact that they are not afraid to be the women God has called them to be. I also said that to let you know I did not cancel my subscription once I read Kinki Freidman's article. The same magazine that made me mad also made me laugh. You just have to know what and what not to take too seriously.

I know that God has a sense of humor, He created me. While I have learned to take personal hygiene very seriously I do not take my looks very seriously. I can't. If I did then I would always be upset. At a very early age I began to suspect that I might be somewhat unsightly. That revelation happened while playing in the sandbox. The kids around me battled with their G.I. Joe while I battled understanding why the cat was trying to bury me.

See, the wisdom of knowing what you should and what you should not take too seriously is a matter of knowing God's word. This kind of wisdom can mean the difference between happiness and sadness, success and failure and even life and death.

This kind of wisdom will make you cheer for your kids instead of yell at the referee. It will cause you to get up on Sunday mornings instead of sleeping. With this kind of wisdom you will find yourself eating a salad for supper while biting into your kid's birthday cake. It's all about priority of importance.

If I know what to take seriously, my mind will be very aware of what God is doing in my life instead of what's going on in the lives of the characters of my favorite television show.

If I know what to take seriously, I will be able to choose the things God wants me to choose the things that are always good for me.

In the early part of the last century the "unsinkable" ship known as the TITANIC set sail from South Hampton, England. When the commander of a nearby ship tried to warn Titanic of a giant ice burg just ahead, the operator's response was chilling.

"Shut up, keep out, you are jamming my signal!"

Because they did not know what they should take seriously, the unsinkable ship was in fact "unsavable." Those on board are not the only people that have been sunk for lack of this wisdom.

Nearly 4000 years before the TITANIC, there was a man by the name of Lott that hailed from a town called Sodom. The angels of God warned Lott and his wife to get out of Sodom and to get out now. Lott's wife decided to prioritize her flaming house over

God's heated warning and it landed her in the biblical Hall of Shame.

We could go on to talk about Samson, the ten foolish virgins and many more, but the bottom line is that there are four words that biblically describe what it means to know what we should take seriously. **The Fear of God!**

In a day full of "No fear" and "Ain't Skeered" bumper stickers we desperately need the balance of this priority. To fear God means to line up your priorities with God's priorities. It means to take what God takes seriously and to dismiss what God does not take seriously.

There is a special blessing for those few folks that will prioritize Him and take Him seriously. And this, we really should take seriously folks.

He will bless those who fear the LORD-- small and great alike.
Psalms 115:13

SOMETHING TO SIP ON:

The Lord takes your life seriously and we ought to take our life in Him seriously as well. One of the ways you can do that is to get sincere and dedicated to His word. You can not say that you respect God if you have no respect for God's word.

His Word is in fact worth taking seriously.

Psalm 19:7-9
"The law of the Lord is perfect ...
the testimony of the Lord is sure ...
the commandment of the Lord is pure ... the judgments of the
Lord are true forever."

Psalm 119:43
"the word of truth."

Psalm 119:142
"Thy law is the truth."

Psalm 119:160
"Thy word is true from the beginning."

John 17:17
"Thy word is truth."

One of the barometers for measuring how committed we are to knowing God is simply taking a look at how serious we are about knowing His word.

How serious of a believer does that make you?

JOHN KNOX AND THE MODERN REFORMATION

Almost 500 years ago there lived a man across the pond in an incredible place called Edinburgh Scotland. I would have never known about him nor would you, unless he had taken the incredible stand that he did in a day when it could have gotten him killed. His name was John Knox.

Being a 6th generation Texan and an 11th generation American that goes all the way back to Jamestown, I just can't help but love a good old fashioned stand against insurmountable odds. A long time before Colonel Travis fired a cannon at Santa Anna and even before General Washington pointed his sword towards Cornwallis, John Knox stood against the established church of his day.

I literally stumbled upon his house on a mission trip to Edinburgh five years ago. In front of an ancient and completely picturesque castle, there is a cobble stone road called "The Royal Mile." Leanna and I were walking down it looking for a place to dodge the cold wind and possibly bite into some haggis, when I passed a door with a metal plaque that read "House of John Knox."

Since then, I have been looking into the life of this great Scottish reformer and let me tell you some things that I have learned.

Born in 1513, John Knox grew up in Scotland and was ordained a priest in his early thirties. He had a personal revival and was converted to Christ after he met two Bible-believing Christians, by the names of Wisehart and Beacon.

Because Wisehart refused to be a part of a political mess directed by the church, he was arrested by the local Catholic Bishop and burned at the stake in 1546. As Knox watched his buddy burn alive he began to hate the established church of his day. It wasn't long after, that the same Bishop had John arrested for suspicion of heresy (meaning that he probably didn't agree with the bishop) and John spent the next 19 months of his life as a galley slave in the dungeon of a ship.

So what is a guy to do when he loves the Lord with all of his heart, yet sees the church as a big mess that he doesn't want to be a part of? He should do what John Knox did, live Jesus and preach Jesus without the okay of the church. You don't make your spiritual walk about church, you make it about Jesus. That was a bold stand then and it still is today.

I wish there were more people like John Knox in our day and age. I wish there were more people that would remain on fire for God even after they are badly hurt by the corporate church. I wish there were more people within the traditional church that would stand up and like John Knox declare-"Our traditions are not necessarily Godly!"

I wish more Pastors and Elders would look at what they are doing and how they are doing it and come to the obvious conclusion that the cloud of God's presence has moved on and they have pitched their tent short of the Promised Land.

I wish there were more congregations that were about the business of building God's Kingdom instead of a personal empire. I wish that the church would quit trying to protect itself from the bad parts of town by moving to the suburbs. Instead I wish that the church would strive to have influence over the decaying parts of our society through serving and reaching out.

The bottom line is that I wish the church would be more like Jesus instead of a professional corporation.

I wonder what John Knox or Martin Luther or Calvin or Tyndale would say about the recognizable church of our day. I wonder if they would see the church as something relevant and life-changing in the cultures of today. I wonder if they would nod their head in approval at the way we are reaching people with the Love of Jesus Christ or if they would speak out against us for trying to build congregations while putting Jesus on the back burner.

I truly wish that it would be okay that our churches were full of teenagers with silly purple hair and ugly piercing in their black painted lips. I wish that old folks would not have to worry about how little their social security checks were because they knew that their church would help them when things got bad.

But what's real is that most churches don't want troublesome teenagers and high maintenance, poor people filling up the pews. Having those people in church would surely run off the good citizens that financially make the corporate machine run efficiently.

I think that the church, as we know it, is preventing the church from being as God wants it. I think there is a real need today for REFORMATION.

I, like a lot of people today, look at the established corporate church as I shake my head and say "I don't think I want to be a part of it." I don't want to be a part of a building committee or a financial board. I want to be a part of a move of God!

With that said I unlike a lot of those same people remain faithful and committed to the calling to the body of Christ that is in my life. I refuse to be bitter or paralyzed. This is not a day to either go with the flow of the mainstream church or to sideline sit and not do anything. It is a day to be where Jesus is and let the rest of the world go where it has always been headed to.

I have decided to be a part of today's Modern Reformation instead of being an armchair quarterback. I am trying to make a difference with out being a part of the problem. John Knox taught me that.

SOMETHING TO SIP ON:

The 4 Pillars of the Reformation:

Christ Alone!
The Bible Alone!
Faith Alone!
Grace Alone!

For more information on the heroes and history of the Reformation I would suggest you check out these websites.

Site on William Tyndale
www.williamtyndale.com

Site on Martin Luther
www.luther.de

Foxes Book of Martyrs on line
www.ccel.org/f/foxe/martyrs/home

Site on the Reformation
www.forerunner.com/forerunner/X0521

Site on the Reformation
www.educ.msu.edu/homepages/laurence/ reformation

Site on the Reformation
www.newgenevacenter.org/west/reformation

Pictures of the Reformists
www.mun.ca/rels/hrollmann/reform/pics/people/ people

One other thing worth mentioning is that when John Knox was 50 years old he decided to marry again after having been a widower for many years. Not only was it a controversy that he married into the same royal family that tried to kill him, but the girl he married was only 17 years old.

HARDLY RECOGNIZABLE
(the first column for the Joshua Star)

These are the confessions of a highly caffeinated Christian. My name is Troy Brewer and this is the introduction of a column called "FRESH FROM THE BREWER." I have been writing this column now for several years and I can't tell you how honored I am to finally be a part of my hometown paper.

This is not the first time I have been in print in the Joshua Star. The first time was in the late 70's when I won the 6th grade U.I.L. poetry reading contest at Joshua Middle School. There I was, in all my radiant glory, with my jeans tucked in my boots, my teeth strung up in braces and my seventies afro looking like a light brown halo. It was a magnificent moment and there was no living with me after that.

So when the editor called me and asked if I could write a column for the J-Town Star, my heart went a little bit 'postal.' You see I am an indigenous Joshua-ite. I have lived here long enough to remember when our hillbilly accents called it "Josh-u-way" instead of the Joshua that everybody says now.

I remember when Burleson was a long way from Joshua and Joshua was a long way from Cleburne. I remember the old water tower near the old part of town and I climbed and wrote my name on it back when it was funny and not a felony to do such things.

I can remember when, from the Dairy Queen parking lot, you could still see the Milky Way in all its spender and the Dairy Queen was the only place in town to eat.

I remember when Julius Reinach died in a car crash at the one red light in town and the entire city showed up at the scene to mourn because everybody knew Mr. Reinach.

Though we have not moved, we do not live in that little place any longer. The sleepy country we used to know and love has given way to the busy metropolis around us and we didn't have to go anywhere to find ourselves under a florescent street lamp.

Like the weather in Texas, if you don't like the area just wait a minute, it'll change. This is the reality of the day we live in and it is the harsh way that progress works. So hang onto your hat, if you still wear one, things are changing and they will continue to change until the return of the King Himself.

Like the town I live in I have also changed in a radical way. The reason I write is not just to rant, but it is to proclaim or to "holler," as the old folks would say, the good news of the person I most love to write about -- me. In May of 1986 I had a personal encounter with Jesus Christ and it was like an atomic bomb went off in my spirit and 'Fresh from the Brewer' is part of the continual fallout.

The Good Lord has taken me on a wild ride over the past 19 years through mission trips in Uganda, Congo, Rwanda,

England, Scotland, Mexico, Costa Rica, Guatemala, Panama, Cuba, Canada and even Israel. I've had the awesome privilege of preaching in over 200 prisons in three of those countries and have even personally spoken to the late Queen Mother of England and the very young King Oyo of Uganda, East Africa.

But in spite of all the traveling, I have never really been able to get away from here. For the past ten years I have had the privilege of pastoring "Open Door Ministries" right here in my old stomping grounds. Because of my rather notorious and tarnished past, I begged God to send me somewhere else but He just wouldn't and for some reason a lot of fine people have been willing to put up with me.

I'm glad that I'm still here and I'm glad that you are also. A lot better people than us didn't make it. That speaks to me of purpose and I can't help but believe that Jesus Christ has a specific calling for our lives and that our best days are not behind us, but ahead.

I am not looking back to the old Joshua or to the old you and me that lived in the old Joshua. If anybody be in Christ he is a new creature as the scripture says and the Lord continues to prove that through those of us that have been able to find Him.

It would be silly and irresponsible of our city leaders to refuse to move forward into the new and they've done a fine job at making this transition. It would also be silly, even tragic, if we refused to change and stayed the same as we were twenty-five years ago.

Just like that, when the apostle Paul looked at his life he put it this way:

....This one thing I do, forgetting those things which are behind, and reaching forth unto those things which are before, I press toward the mark for the prize of the high calling of God in Christ Jesus. **Philippians 3:13**

Paul decided he didn't want a rerun. He wanted something better and he found all he was looking for in the person of Jesus Christ. If you are looking for something better, Jesus is perfect for you. He wants to make your life look like the new city of Joshua, a place that has come so far you won't even recognize it anymore.

I look forward to our weekly sips of wisdom from the Carpenter's cup and am glad to know that you are still moving forward after all these years.

SOMETHING TO SIP ON:

This was the first column in the Joshua Star and as you can see, I was really excited about the opportunity to be in the local paper.

This whole theme of moving forward and letting God change you is something that I preach all the time.

If there is not change then our encounters with the Lord are worthless.

Romans 12:2
"And be not conformed to this world: but be ye transformed by the renewing of your mind, that ye may prove what is that good, and acceptable, and perfect, will of God."

HEARING AID

On the night of June 25, 1993, Brenda Davis went into labor six weeks early. After a complicated delivery, her son Terrell was born without a heartbeat. "They took him away to be resuscitated before I could see him," she said. Davis was relieved when she finally saw the boy in the neonatal ward, but a new problem was very evident: "I saw that he only had one ear."

Terrell was born with "unilateral microtia," a birth defect that stops ear formation. For the first eleven years of young Terrell's life, he only had one ear, the left, in which he was totally deaf, and then some bumpy skin where his right ear should have been.

The good news is that though there wasn't an outside ear, there was an ear drum and he could slightly hear muffled sounds from that right side. Terrell communicated through sign language and learned to read lips and body language but that was the extent of his communication skills. His defect had left Terrell incredibly shy. He stayed away from the other kids "and he wouldn't attempt to speak with anyone until he was very comfortable," said Brenda. "People on the bus would gasp and point trying to get a look at his bad ear," Brenda said. "It made him very uncomfortable."

Brenda, being a single mom and with very little money, had great difficulty in paying for his speech therapy lessons. In all of her struggles she never imagined that there was a surgery that could reconstruct Terrell an ear and literally "heal" him of the deafness they had known for so many years.

She didn't know and dared not hope for something that she couldn't afford anyway.

Enter Dr. Thomas Romo, a major hospital's Chief of Facial Plastic Surgery and the president and founder of the nonprofit Little Baby Face Foundation, which helps children with facial deformities. "I saw Terrell for the first time, and I thought, wow, no one's taken the time to help this kid," says Romo. "He's almost deaf, and he doesn't have to be."

After several reconstructive surgeries for the outside of his ear, Terrell had a good looking ear to match the other one. However, the greatest miracle took place after an ear canal had been formed and an implant had been made specifically for him. With mom in the room the devise was turned on and Dr. Romo whispered behind him. "Hey, Terrell, how are you doing?"

Terrell's face lit up like a Christmas tree and for the first time he could hear and hear really well.

Brenda Davis, Romo's nurse, and Dr. Romo himself all began crying. "It was infectious," he said. "You could see how amazed he really was."

You know, it's really hard to hear when you don't have an ear. Spiritually Jesus Christ deals with this kind of problem every day of the week.

A lot of people do not know it but there is a miracle that can take place in every individual's life so they can "hear" what the voice of the Lord is specifically saying to their heart on a very personal level.

The problem is that most people don't want to have that deep of a relationship with Him. They would prefer to just stay in contact with or read books written by people that do.

The Bible says in Genesis that when Adam and Eve heard the voice of the LORD, God walking in the garden in the cool of the day, they hid themselves amongst the trees of the garden, away from the presence of the LORD God.

Things haven't changed much since then. When you get tuned into the true voice of God you are either going to fall down at His feet and get with His program or you are going to try and hide yourself behind something. It is the nature of fallen people to hide themselves from the voice of God but it is the nature of godly people to listen and to follow His voice. Jesus said,

My sheep hear my voice, and I know them, and they follow me:
John 10:27

Our ability to follow him is dependent upon our ability to hear His voice. I am not talking about an audible voice. I am not telling you that I get up in the mornings, drink coffee with Jesus and discuss the sports page. I am talking about the God given ability to tune our hearts into His heart and to be spiritually led by His will for our lives.

SOMETHING TO SIP ON:

Romans 10:17
So then faith cometh by hearing,
and hearing by the word of God.

In this verse Paul is not talking about physical hearing. He is referring to a spiritual ability to hear. If it is strictly physical then deaf people could never have faith. That's not the case. I am telling you that today you can know God and have more hope and more joy then you have ever had in your life by simply increasing your ability to hear His voice in a greater way then you have ever heard Him.

Just stop what you are doing and humble yourself. Ask the Lord to speak to your heart and make Him known to you personally. The "still and small" voice that is described in 1st Kings is not just a description of the voice of God; it is also a description of the Heart that is able to recognize His voice. Make sure that you are not too busy and too big to be able to hear what God is trying to speak into your life.

Brother Terrell couldn't hear because he didn't have an ear and I fear that a lot of us Christians are spiritually just like that.

Or as Jesus put it in **Revelation 2:7,** *"He that hath an ear, let him hear what the Spirit saith unto the churches..."*

NO STRINGS ATTACHED

What do Ronald Reagan, Oscar de la Hoya and Leonardo da Vinci have in common with Joan of Arc, Fidel Castro and David Letterman? Besides being names that we might recognize, the answer I am looking for is that they are all left handed people.

One out of every ten people walking down the street is a lefty. Everywhere they go; left-handed people come across tools designed for right-handed folks. From scissors to camcorders to screw drivers to hockey sticks and baseball gloves; lefties learn early that they need to develop special skills to live in a right-handed world.

Medical researchers have searched long and hard for what causes people to be left-handed. The researchers have concluded that left-handed people are left-handed for the same reason as some people can touch their nose with their tongue. It's just one of those things that shows up in about ten percent of the population. (By the way, I can wiggle my ears. Ha!)

Two of the four BEATLES were left-handed (Paul & Ringo) as were both of the Everly Brothers. Peter Benchley wrote the book "JAWS" with his left hand and Michelangelo painted every masterpiece one stroke at a time, with a brush between his little left fingers.

Now the cool thing about Michelangelo is that he was in fact ambidextrous. He could paint with either hand. When one hand got tired, he switched to the other and just kept right on painting. I think that's so cool when people can do that.

British artist, Sir Edwin Henry Landseer (1802-1873) could draw with both hands simultaneously. He's famous for painting a horse's head with one hand and a stag's head with the other - - at the same time before an audience of pupils. This same guy taught drawing and etching to Queen Victoria who was also a lefty that later became ambidextrous. Benjamin Franklin was ambidextrous and signed the Declaration of Independence and the Constitution with his left hand.

Our 20th president, James Garfield was a well educated backwoodsman born in a log cabin but with an exceptional talent given from the Lord. Although he could write with either hand with equal ease, he could also write Greek with his left hand and Latin with his right hand simultaneously while carrying on a conversation in English!

I can barely write Texan which sometimes doesn't even count as English and I can't even do that if the TV is on.

Ambidexterity or the ability to use both hands equally well is a visible parable of a very real spiritual principle. Jesus talks about the importance of it and warns us to get it right in **Matthew Chapter Six**.

When you do a charitable deed you shouldn't let your right hand know what the left hand is doing that your charitable

deed may be in secret; and your Father who sees in secret
will Himself reward you openly
(NKJV)

There has been a lot of debate throughout the centuries as to exactly what Jesus was saying when He said that we should be full of Spiritual Ambidexterity.

The ability to do one thing with your right hand and do something completely different with your left hand is not an easy thing to accomplish even if it is only figuratively speaking.

I know that one of the ways we could interpret this comes from focusing on the part about the alms or the charitable deed. The picture is that while you are giving something with your right hand you are holding out your left hand to get something back. That's a bad thing and in this case we are in fact commanded to not let our left hand know what our right hand is doing.

If you do something for somebody, especially when it comes to charitable giving, do it without any strings attached.

Last week, several hundred Christians gathered together to give away over 37,000 pounds of food to some of Johnson Counties needy in Cleburne, Texas. Open Door Ministries teamed up with Pastor Pearly Brown and the wonderful people at Emanuel Temple and you have never seen so many hugs in one place in all of your life. Over 1100 people came out to get food, clothes, professional haircuts and an encouraging word.

In all the time, talent and treasure that all of us spent, do you know what we required of the recipients that we blessed? Nothing! Absolutely nada, zilch, zero, zip. We didn't charge them a dime; we didn't require church attendance or make them learn the secret handshake. We gave and did not receive anything.

That's the way it is supposed to be when you do charitable giving. You give, not expecting to receive from that person that you are giving to, but from the Father which Jesus promised, will reward us openly. We are not out there trying to market our churches, we are trying to evangelize for the Kingdom of Heaven and make the love of Jesus Christ famous.

If you do something for somebody, whether they are your next door neighbor, or someone you don't even know, do it as unto the Lord and without any strings attached. Release people of any obligation of owing you anything for any deed that you have done for them in the love of God. A gift with strings attached is not a gift it is a bribe.

Don't let your left hand know what your right hand is doing and trust that the Lord knows and He will never forget.

SOMETHING TO SIP ON:

While the world accuses Americans of being selfish empire builders, when it comes to charitable giving, no other country even comes close. Americans are the most generous people in the world.

Even in a difficult economic year like 2002, allaboutgod.com says charitable giving still rose 5% to $241 billion. In fact, charitable giving was 2.3% of the U.S. GNP, exceeding 2% for the first time since 1971. Remarkably, this increase came after the greatest two-year equity market decline in U.S. history.

As cool as that is, I know that a lot of those awesome givers did not get what they could have had out of giving like that, because they sought a reward other than the Lord.

God doesn't just love a giver. The Bible says He loves a cheerful giver and one that doesn't have an ulterior motive.

When you give, do so because it is your privilege to give and leave it in your service to the Lord. There are a lot of people that would give but can't because they have nothing in the world to give away. We really are privileged to be able to be someone that gives without strings attached.

STRANGE DAYS

It's time once again for confessions from a caffeinated Christian in this column that we call 'Fresh from the Brewer.' The struggle of course is to come up with something interesting since brilliant is obviously out of the question. However, this column serves far more than just the reader's edification; sometimes it makes for a very good "rant" from the Brewer himself.

Ladies and Gentlemen buckle your seat belts the rant will now begin.

The headlines of the past two weeks have looked more like the titles of a Sponge Bob Marathon than actual captions. It's official; we live on a very strange planet.

"Python Bursts after trying to eat Alligator" A 13-foot Burmese python recently burst after it apparently tried to swallow a live, six-foot alligator whole, authorities said in Miami Florida. Oh that's good, just when you thought it was safe to swim in the swamp.

"Police find Naked Burglar" Police responding to an alarm at a cash advance business in Darlington, South Carolina, say they found a naked man hanging from the ceiling.

In Texas, we tend to shoot our burglars. I can only imagine what we would do to a naked man hiding in our rafters. Rob me if you must but don't force me to see you uncovered in my attic. I've had enough traumas in my life and I just don't need to deal with that in my head.

"Mistake leads to 29-cent Gas Price" Motorists in Lincoln, Nebraska, took advantage of a mistake made by a store manager and for 30 to 45 minutes, three of a Convenience Store's four pumps sold premium unleaded gas for 29 cents a gallon.

As news of the cheap fuel spread, lines formed at the store, said Max Wolfe, who was doing landscaping for the stores. Wolfe and his co-workers took time out to fill up. "I was on E, and I filled my tank up for $4," Wolfe said. "It made my day."

Yeah, that's the kind of guy you want working for you. If there's a major malfunction, why warn you about it when he can exploit your weakness and legally steal from you. I would say that Wolfe would be an appropriate name for this brother.

"Son and Embalmed Mother buried Together" The Associated Press reported that in Hyderabad India, a man who kept the embalmed body of his mother at home in a glass casket for 21 years was finally buried along with her after his death.

Hundreds of residents on Sunday attended the burials of Syed Abdul Ghafoor, 69, and his mother at a mosque in Siddavata, a town 300 miles south of Hyderabad the capital of Andhra Pradesh state.

"I fulfilled the last wish of my uncle. He had told us that his mother's body should be buried only after his death," said his nephew, Syed Noor.

Now there's a story worth printing! Some nut across the pond keeps his mom propped up in the living room the same way I do my ten point buck and not just for a week or two but for twenty-one years. Imagine what this did for his marriage!

I just have this picture of sitting on this guy's couch and sipping my Dr. Pepper while his mummified mother lay quietly in her glass coffee table at my feet. How awkward is that?

On top of all this, his hillbilly family is so naive that they all go along with it as if this is what you are supposed to do when mama meets her maker.

Ladies and gentlemen Elvis has left the building!

You had better pony up, cowboy because know it or not, the world around you is crazy and you are required to have a right mind anyway. Unless you live like a hermit, there is no way you can escape the madness of the day we live in. I push my cart through the Wal-Mart parking lot the way Indiana Jones ran through the temple of Doom because I understand that at any given moment, anybody around me can lose their ever-lovin' mind. We live and operate among people that bring clear definition to the word "instability" and in a day defined the same way.

So how is a guy supposed to be steady in an unstable world? It's all about who you know.

Three thousand years ago, a poet-warrior and shepherd-King named David lived a progressive life full of contradiction. In spite of His incredible instability and the constant turbulence of the day he lived in, David thrived in unwavering security. He was full of peace in the midst of uproar. He was bold and confident when he should have been terrified. David had his act together when everything else was falling apart.

It's this same David who prayed the following prayer in the book of Psalms

Hear my cry, O God; attend unto my prayer.
From the end of the earth will I cry unto thee,
when my heart is overwhelmed,
lead me to the rock that is higher than I.
For thou hast been a shelter for me,
and a strong tower from the enemy.
I will abide in thy tabernacle for ever:
I will trust in the covert of thy wings.
Psalms 61:1-4

The world is crazy and you need Jesus! Let the Spirit of the Lord lead you to the Rock (Jesus Christ: the very definition of stability) that is indeed higher than you. He is above the muck and the mire that all of us deal with. Let Him lead you my friend, into His Shelter, His Protection and into His trust.

Cry out to Him and let the good news of His Gospel be real in your life in spite of the headlines. The peace that passes understanding is still available to you but you've got to meet the Prince of Peace to get it. Reach out to Jesus and find Him fast because these really are strange days and next week will be even more bizarre.

SOMETHING TO SIP ON:

Some really good websites for strange news are: www.davesdaily. com abclocal.go.com/wls/**news/strange/** www.msnbc.com/comics/nw.asp or you can just go to your web browser and type in "weird news bizarre."

There is an untold number of weirdness out there and it is piling up by the minute. The only thing that God tells us not to think strange is that we go though trials and tribulations. This is familiar territory for a real Christian.

Beloved, think it not strange concerning the
fiery trial which is to try you,
as though some strange thing happened unto you:
But rejoice, inasmuch as ye are partakers
of Christ's sufferings; that, when his glory shall be revealed,
ye may be glad also with exceeding joy.
1 Peter 4:12-13

See there, you are not the weirdo everybody says you are.

NINE GOOD REASONS NOT TO BE THANKFUL

Luke 17:11
And it came to pass, as he went to Jerusalem,
that he passed through the midst of Samaria and Galilee.
And as he entered into a certain village, there met him ten men
that were lepers, which stood afar off:
And they lifted up their voices,
and said, Jesus, Master, have mercy on us.
And when he saw them, he said unto them,
Go show yourselves unto the priests. And it came to pass,
that, as they went, they were cleansed.
And one of them, when he saw that he was healed,
turned back, and with a loud voice glorified God,
And fell down on his face at his feet, giving him thanks:
and he was a Samaritan.
And Jesus answering said, Were there not ten cleansed?
but where are the nine?
There are not found that returned to give glory to God,
save this stranger.
And he said unto him, Arise, go thy way:
thy faith hath made thee whole.

I love how the Bible throws little subtle things into a story that gently fall on us as soft revelation and then hits your heart like a meat cleaver. This story tells us that Jesus was "on his way" to Jerusalem — and to the cross. Traveling between Samaria and Judea, He passed near a leper colony. He was by now becoming famous and ten of the lepers called out to Him "Jesus, Master, have mercy on us!"

Jesus, being Jesus stopped what He was doing and said to the ten guys with leprosy *"Go and show yourselves to the priests."*

As they left, a miracle happened and they were healed of their terrible disease. All of the lepers obeyed Jesus' command to ***"go and show yourselves to the priests."*** All ten of them were healed and went home to mama while only one returned to Jesus to say "thank you."

Only one stopped what he was doing, put his plans on hold and said "I've got to tell Jesus how much I appreciate what He has done for me."

In the style of good storytellers, Luke gives us the punch line at the end of the story — *"And he was a Samaritan."* That despised foreigner, the hated alien, the uncouth reject was the only one who really was thankful.

A lot of times it's like that. The people you think would really get it, often do not. And those you think won't, get it better than most.

I have come up with an idea of what happened to the other nine and why they were not thankful. See if any of this sounds familiar to you.

(1) **The 1ˢᵗ guy was just too busy and he thought he would get to Jesus later.** If you don't have Jesus high on your list of priorities, you will consistently be unthankful. His kid's soccer games and his never ending work schedules probably kept him way too busy to stop and be truly thankful.

(2) **The 2ⁿᵈ fellow wanted to wait and see if his healing would last.** A lack of trust breeds un-thankfulness.

(3) **The 3ʳᵈ one decided he never actually had leprosy to begin with.** He reckoned that it wasn't that Jesus had actually done something for him; it was just that he had come out of a hard time and he had been confused. I've known people that have come out of unbelievably terrible things. The Lord gave them what they had been praying for: a completely different vocation or a new marriage with a wonderful spouse that doesn't cheat and when He does, they go right back to the world and are never thankful. Because they minimize the mess that God brought them out of they minimize the Miracle that Jesus did and therefore they are not thankful.

(4) **The 4ᵗʰ one decided that he would have gotten well anyway.** Why give God credit for something that might have happened anyway?

(5) **The 5ᵗʰ one wasn't thankful because he decided that it was the priest that healed him.** Why give God credit for something a preacher can do?

(6) **The 6ᵗʰ one never was thankful because once He thought about it; he came to the conclusion that Jesus didn't really do anything. "He just told me what to do and I am the one that healed me."** Why give God credit for something that I have had to work hard on myself?

(7) **The 7ᵗʰ one thought "Any rabbi could have done it."** He chalked it up to a generic religious experience. Why give Jesus credit for something any religion can do?

(8) **The 8ᵗʰ one never got thankful because instead of focusing on his healing, he constantly thought about all the bad things that happened while he was sick.** Why give Jesus credit for a healing when you can't forget about the disease He has healed you from?

(9) **The 9th fellow didn't have any bad intentions; it just never occurred to him that he should be thankful.** He, like a wild animal is simply consumed with his own passions and his own fears and it never occurs to him once to humble himself to the one who has given him life. There are a lot of people in our county that are exactly this. Sometimes, the fellow typing this is the worst of all us.

When I think about the Samaritan leper I can't help but tip my hat at him. Surely he, like the others, had family obligations to meet, friendships to renew, things that had to be done. Yet, he, and only he, returned to Jesus and really was thankful.

Thankfulness is more than an act of good manners. It is a willingness to take yourself down as the God of your life and put Jesus up as the God of your life. I hope that you can throw out all the reasons you can find not to be thankful. Look up from this paper to the Father that sees you and live a life that truly says "Thank you."

SOMETHING TO SIP ON:

One of the secrets of a successful Christian life is acknowledging that there is always something to be thankful for. Sometimes those things are hard to see but they are always there. God doesn't ask us to be thankful *"FOR"* everything. He commands us to be thankful *"IN"* everything.

Being thankful is more of a condition of the heart rather than an assessment of your situation.

One of the "tricks" to being thankful in hard times is growing in the ability to know the truth over the facts. The facts of every situation are real and not to be ignored but they do not supersede the truth. What I mean is, the facts change from moment to moment but the truth abides forever.

Christians do not live according to facts they live according to truth.

The fact of the matter is that I might have the rug pulled out from under me from time to time but the truth is that I am standing on the rock.

The fact is that I don't know what I am going to do sometimes but the truth is that God knows everything and I trust in that truth in spite of the facts.

Knowing the truth sets me free from the curse of only knowing the facts.

John 8:32
You shall know the truth and the truth will make you free

RUNNING A PATIENT RACE

According to Webster an *oxymoron* is a phrase using two words that contradict each other as they describe something that may not be a contradiction at all. I recently have been pondering the use of many an oxymoron being used in Americana today. See if you recognize any of these:

"Government Organization" No doubt that within the government there are organizations, but how organized do you think they really are? Call any of the hard working people down at the drivers license place and talk to one of the few employees where there should be a couple of dozen and see if they think their government organization is in fact organized.

"Personal Computer" I have never met a computer that was actually personal. I am as nice as I can be to mine but it is rarely nice back to me. I think a more proper term would be my cold and impersonal computer.

"Living Dead" These words will try and wreck your theology. The living is not among the dead nor is the dead living. The

living are living and the dead are dead and I am not living like I'm dead and why should I when I am living?

"Same Difference" Something heard in the vernacular of Johnson County every day. You go to the oil changing place and you say, "Should I get Pennzoil or Valvoline?" and the feller shrugs his shoulders, spits on the ground and says "Same difference."

"Taped Live" Is it live or is it Memorex? It has to be one or the other because if it is taped then it is not live.

"Plastic Glasses" If your glasses are plastic then why don't we just call them plastics?

"Tight Slacks" A lot of folk's slacks are getting tighter all the time and your slacks might not be as slack as they were first advertised.

"Pretty Ugly" For those of us that are ugly, we don't even want to bring up the subject. If you are out there talking about how ugly I am, don't describe me as **"pretty ugly,"** you should say really ugly and leave the word pretty out altogether.

"Dodge Ram" I drive a truck and it cracks me up that my Dodge is called a ram. Really, it's the perfect title for my truck because I will dodge you if you get into my lane and probably ram you if I get into yours.

"Jumbo Shrimp" A shrimp is something little but a jumbo shrimp is a great big little something.

"Microsoft Works" This is a matter of opinion for some folks. I am actually a really big fan of Microsoft, but works doesn't necessarily work all the time. Sometimes works would work if the worker himself knew how to work the dang thing.

In the biblical book of Hebrews there is a great chapter with an incredible verse that also has an oxymoron. It says,

Wherefore seeing we also are compassed about with so great a
cloud of witnesses, let us lay aside every weight,
and the sin which doth so easily beset us,
and let us run with patience the race that is set before us,
Hebrews 12:1

Did you catch it? It's just under the second piece of "lettuce." There is "let us" lay aside the weight, a great verse to put on your refrigerator and then there is "let us" run with patience. Now there is another term to add to your oxymoron list; A patient race."

How can you run a race and be patient? The race that the Lord has ordered you and me to run is not a sprint where we are in a hurry to get somewhere, but it is in fact a test of endurance and more about long term and big distance. The finish line for us is not about being the fastest or the smartest or the best athlete, it is about being what the Bible calls an "over-comer." Not only are we supposed to over come this world though Jesus Christ but we are supposed to patiently help those around us to make it to the same finish line.

One of my favorite secular charities is a name that you will recognize called the Special Olympics. They provide year round sports training and athletic competition for mentally disabled people throughout the world.

A few years back a televised competition showed the perfect example of what it means to run a patient race. With the "pop" of a starter gun, about a dozen special athletes took off running. They didn't get very far before one of them stumbled and fell and sat in his lane crying in disappointment.

One of the other athletes, a beautiful young lady with Downs Syndrome, turned back to help her fellow runner and encourage him to get back up. When the other runners saw her compassion, they stopped running as well and the crowd cheered as all of them crossed the finish line together.

I believe it was a living illustration of the Word of God in action. Let us run the race but let us do it with patience for those around us that fall and get hurt on the way. I pray that we as the body of Christ have the wisdom of that young lady in the Special Olympics to understand that it is not about the competition but about overcoming the things that would keep us from finishing the race at all.

To him that overcometh will I grant to sit with me in my throne,
even as I also overcame,
and am set down with my Father in his throne.
He that hath an ear,
let him hear what the Spirit saith unto the churches.
Revelation 3:21-22

SOMETHING TO SIP ON:

When you are working your way through the Book of Revelation you are not going to get very far before you come across the words of Jesus and the promises to those that "over come."

The context of this phrase comes in Christ's words, through John, to the church at Sardis— the dead church; Philadelphia— a humble church with no word of reproof; and the church at Laodicea—the lukewarm church with big time problems.

The Greek word for "overcome" is *nikao* which means "to subdue, conquer, overcome, prevail, or get the victory."

Three times in Chapter three, in vs. 5, 12, and 21, is the phrase *"he who overcomes"* and then the promises that follow.

It's important to keep in mind that you are called an over comer even when you are feeling like an under achiever. Again you are called an "over comer."

This should be the desire, the goal and the mandate of every born again Christian. May we not ball up and shut down or give in and freak out but continue in His grace, past that finish line.

TAKE ME TO YOUR LEADER

Roswell, New Mexico seems to be a modern day Mecca for "Weirdoes." Every conspiracy theory and alien abduction story that you have ever heard has found a safe haven in Roswell. It's just a good place to call home if you are into the X-files.

Not that I don't like a good weirdo because I am a classic example of one myself. Now I typically can't stand conspiracy theories and I don't go around looking for crop circles but there have been sightings of me at Star Wars conventions.

Speaking of Star Wars, it is a fact that my very dear cousin Angie is married to Peter Mayhew. Peter is the British born actor that plays Chewbacca in the Star Wars movies. I have had the privilege of meeting Mr. Mayhew and he is a very nice guy. That makes me the only Pastor in America that can honestly say that I am kin to Chewbacca the Wookie. For those of you that know me I bet you are not surprised.

As far as pastors go, I'm weird in that category too. I just don't fit into the typical pastor mold. I suspect that a lot of pastors feel this way but in my case it is completely legitimate.

In another weird way I'm a lot like Roswell. I seem to be a sort of a magnet for strange and even generally crazy people. My wife can't understand it but it is a fact that very eccentric and unsociable people tend to migrate towards me.

People who know me know that the reason I do not hand the microphone over to people that want to give a testimony in my church services is because about five years ago we had a "Roswell moment."

Her testimony was that Jesus had saved her and that since then she had ceased to have monthly visitations from the "Fire Aliens" in her back pasture.

I can remember looking out into the audience and seeing people whisper to each other, "What did she say?" as I politely took back the microphone before she could finish her "testimony."

I said something like "Praise the Lord for her breakthrough." And then I proceeded to act like nothing else had happened. I mean, you can get away with things in Johnson County that you can't in Highland Park, but even this was a little too much.

According to the Sci-Fi flicks of the nineteen fifties when an alien shows up they demand that you take them to the higher authority by saying "Take me to your leader." What's real is that on the planet we live on, we Christians are the weirdoes and we are supposed to be taking the world to our Leader. If you can wrap your head around it, we are the ones that are "not of this world" and the Bible even calls us "Aliens."

Jesus told the religious leaders of his day ....*Ye are from beneath; I am from above: ye are of this world; I am not of this world.* **John 8:23**

We are supposed to be leading people to Jesus and giving people access to his love and his life changing power the same way that Jesus has led us to the Father. We have no access to the father except by Him.

Donald G. Barnhouse once wrote a story about President Lincoln in his book "God's River." The story illustrates this access we are supposed to be introducing to people.

Following the Civil War, a dejected Confederate soldier was sitting outside the grounds of the White House. A young boy approached him and inquired why he was so sad.

The solider related how he had repeatedly tried to see President Lincoln to tell him why he was unjustly deprived of certain lands in the South following the war. On each occasion as he attempted to enter the White House, the guards crossed their bayoneted guns in front of the door and turned him away.

The boy motioned to the old soldier to follow him. When they approached the entrance, the guards came to attention, stepped back and opened the door for the boy. He proceeded to the library where the President was resting and introduced the soldier to his father.

The boy was Tad Lincoln. The soldier had gained an audience with the President through the President's son.

Just like that, it is through Jesus, *God's only begotten Son* **(John 3:16)** that we have access to *God, our heavenly Father* **(John 14:6)**.

That might make us look like we are a little bit off the beaten path, but that is what we should be about - taking the world to our leader.

SOMETHING TO SIP ON:

It's not about trying to get people to come to our church. It can't be about trying to make people understand the Bible.

True evangelism is all about connecting people to the Lord and to His Kingdom.

If we are not hooking people up with their own personal relationship with God through Jesus Christ, completely free and independent of us, then we are about someone else's business.

THE REASON FOR THE RISEN

A Sunday school teacher was attempting to teach her young students the true meaning of Easter. "Why do we celebrate Easter?" she asked. When the children replied, "Because of the Easter bunny, Easter eggs, candy, spring, etc.," she said, "No. Those are Easter traditions and symbols, but what is the REASON why we celebrate Easter? What happened at the very first Easter?"

A little girl raised her hand and said, "Easter celebrates Jesus coming out of the tomb." "Yes!" said the teacher excited and relieved that finally the correct answer had surfaced. Encouraged, she prompted, "Jesus arose from the tomb, and what does He do for us?" The kiddo replied, "He looks to see if he can see his shadow, and if He can, he goes back in for another six weeks."

It's so easy to mess up the whole big deal of the importance of resurrection and to just blend it with other traditions and myths. It's a lot like what happens when a McDonalds goes up on a corner in town. Within a year or two you will find a Burger King, Taco bell and a KFC on the other three corners connected to it.

If you put an Outback Steakhouse on the Highway in a remote location, within a year they will rename that area "Restaurant Row" and it will look like the Vegas strip with competing eating places. It is not very long after, that your very special place is just one more house to eat a steak in.

The celebration of the resurrection of Jesus Christ is just like that. The same person that respects the day we honor the resurrection can also make a pilgrimage to the Alamo every March and cry the same tears that he does on Good Friday. After a while, the day we sadly know as Easter becomes just one more competing holiday in a long line on Spiritual Restaurant Row.

Some genius named Constantine started this mess a long time ago. In a Michael Jackson "We are the World" attempt to unite the Pagans and Christians of his day, Constantine combined the celebration of Christian holidays with the local myths and Pagan rituals; and before long the powerful revelation of the Gospel of Jesus became just another nice idea.

Listen up, reader! The Resurrection of Jesus Christ is not just another nice idea. It's the greatest hope that the world has ever been offered. Jesus didn't just get up after He assumed room temperature; He slapped death in the face. He beat death down after He himself had been beaten to a bloody pulp.

Like Saddam Hussein having his matted, nasty hair combed through for bugs on world wide television, death was shown not to be as undefeatable as had been advertised. In one brilliant stroke Jesus humbled and humiliated Death, Hell and the Grave. Then He added insult to injury by having women be the first to publish the news in a totally male dominated world.

Resurrection power is more than having fun with kids and looking for Easter eggs. I am not against that, but God help us to not diminish the greatest event in human history for the sake of our own silly traditions.

A lot of church folk have taken resurrection off the front burner the way they send their elderly mother to the back room when company comes to call. Instead of focusing on the power of overcoming death, for fear they may be embarrassed somehow, they say nice things like "Easter is about learning how to cope with death." That we can, "face death without fear, with courage and dignity." I heard a TV preacher say that last week and I nearly lost my lunch.

Big deal, I screamed back at the one eyed beast in my living room. Philosophers, poets, and scientists can do that. I remember the astronomer Carl Sagan mentioned in an interview that he was looking forward to death as "the last great adventure." Well I hope that his last adventure turned out better than Custer's last adventure.

Upon the death of Lincoln, Walt Whitman wrote a beautiful poem entitled, "When Lilacs Last in the Dooryard Bloom'd." Whitman wrestled with the thought of death in his verses. In the end, he decided that all we can do is embrace it like a friend: "Come, sweet, soothing death. Undulate around me, arriving, arriving." What a fool! Well, he can have death if he so desires it and even be its friend if he wants to, but don't count me among the friends of death. I am a friend of life and His name is Jesus! In fact death ought to hate me. I expect that when it is my time to go, that death will spit at me as I spit right back and remind him that he was defeated at the empty tomb of Jesus 2000 years ago.

Whitman's contemporary, the poet William Cullen Bryant wrote what some have called the most beautiful American poem, "Thanatopsis," (which is Greek for "A View of Death"). And what was his view of death? In beautiful, flowing verse with elegant words, his bottom line was that the best we can hope for is that our body, placed in the earth, will by its decay help some other form of life spring forth. Our death helps produce life.

I'm sorry Mr. Brilliant philosopher, no matter how elegant your language, that message puts people on Prozac. Not only is your body fertilizer but so are your words. It leaves me very unimpressed with how fascinated you are with death when you don't pay attention to the God that has conquered death for your sake!

God has so much more planned for us than merely to be fertilizer for ferns. That doesn't dignify human beings. Jesus, however, gives us the highest dignity; He rose from death as our REDEEMER TO GIVE YOU ETERNAL VICTORY.

SOMETHING TO SIP ON:

Three years ago I had the privilege of getting to go to Jerusalem. Before I stepped into that famous garden tomb I turned to my wife and said, "Leanna, I am going to be highly disappointed if the body of Jesus is in there."

I was not disappointed and neither will you be if you can trust in Jesus. Take my word for it. He is not there. He is really is risen.

A RUDE DUDE IN A CRUDE MOOD

The cool thing about doing so much mission work is you find your self in places you never imagined. Over the past few years I have had the privilege of visiting a lot of different countries and cultures.

Now the problem is, you can also find yourself in real hot water by not being up to speed on what the locals consider rude behavior. Since I love to eat so much, a big part of my traveling experiences have to do with the food and I tell you, there are lots of different cultural "dos and don'ts" that go along with the food on the plate.

Yes I know better than to put my big, corn fed foot on the table! Even though I am sure some of you right here in Johnson County have no problem with that at all. But do you know that in China it is considered an insult if you eat everything on the plate? The way they figure it, you are saying that the person serving the food did not give you enough to eat. Now I have observed that most Chinese men are too skinny and I suspect this tradition might have something to do with it.

This code of conduct would not go over well in Texas. It never occurs to us to stop eating until there is nothing left on the plate. For us, a diet means getting a smaller plate at the Golden Corral.

In Canada, the Inuit people say "thank you" after the meal by burping out loud and it is considered rude if you do not burp. Now this code of conduct goes over very well in Texas. I have seen it myself at the end of church functions here in Johnson County.

In Uganda, you do not beckon the waitress, or anybody for that matter, by putting you hand palm up, like we do, while opening and closing your hand. This is considered unbelievably vulgar behavior and has something to do with picking up prostitutes. You don't want to do this especially if you are planning on preaching that evening to anyone that doesn't think you are a pervert.

I'll tell you something I think is rude and that's when you talk to someone and they don't talk back. I mean, if I say, "Hello," to a stranger I expect a polite response. This is why I don't do well in places like New York and especially London.

In London, you can be on a subway that is packed like sardines with people and still hear a pin drop because no one will acknowledge that there is anyone else in the world besides themselves. Yeah sure, your face is in my armpit and his knee is in my back and we are all playing twister without the big dots on the floor, but it is better in the English psyche, if we never even say hello to each other. The Brits blow my mind with their strange culture of being isolated in the midst of millions of other people. That's just rude I think and I can't help but talk to them anyway.

One time I was on a train in London and my knees were touching this other guy's knees seated in front of me. I said "Hello," and he just blankly stared at me. At first I thought he didn't hear me so I said, "Did you have a hard day at work?" This stuffy old goat just leaned back, folded his arms and tilted his nose a little higher in disgust. In response I began to have a conversation with him, wherein I answered myself in what I imagined his voice would sound like. He sat there listening to me un-amused.

"So, hard day at the office?" I said in my voice.

"Just bloody terrible." I said in his voice with a hateful attitude. "I've got a bad tooth in the back of my head and it's really giving me problems."

"Oh, I'm sorry," I said in my voice. "Have you been to the pharmacy?" "No," I said in his voice. "I'm a bad alcoholic and drugs make my lips swell up."

At that, the man called me an ugly name and got up to move to another chair. "Oh you can speak." I said as he pushed his way through several people. "I win! Made ya talk!"

My poor wife was embarrassed but I was amused. I am still laughing about it and it makes for great preaching material.

I would like to tell you that Jesus Christ took time to speak to people even when it was considered culturally "incorrect" to do so. The Bible says when He spoke to the Samaritan woman at the well the people were amazed the two were talking at all. If the Bible didn't state otherwise I would think that Jesus was in England instead of Israel.

I would also like to tell you that He is still speaking today. He is not rude and doesn't mind getting involved in your every day life. I encourage you today to take the time to stop and listen to the voice of the Lord in your heart. God is speaking to you but like people on a London subway, most folks choose to tune God out and act like He is not even there. That's just plain rude but it is the way that people are, even here in Texas.

For God speaketh once, Yea twice,
though man regardeth it not.
Job 33:14 (ASV)

SOMETHING TO SIP ON:

Just because God is speaking doesn't mean that you know it and just because you know it doesn't men that you understand it.

In the book of 1ˢᵗ Kings, Elijah covers his face when he hears the voice of God and it is described as "still" and "small."

Still and small is not only a description of God voice, I believe it also a description of the Heart that is able to hear God's voice.

Let us make sure that we are not too big and too busy to really get a bead on what our master is saying.

GOD'S ORDER TO BE OBSESSIVE COMPULSIVE

As you sip on this week's cup of Jehovah Java, I want to give you some recent American Music History.

A few years back, four young guys with a little bit of talent and a whole lot of charisma painted their faces, stuck out their tongues, stomped on a few baby chickens and took the rock and roll world by storm.

They called themselves KISS and if you haven't heard their racket I bet at some time you have seen their unsightly image, because while they were not necessarily great musicians they were indeed, and still are in fact, marketing geniuses.

When I was a kid, you could not look anywhere without seeing KISS merchandise and collectables. Kids traded in Scooby Doo lunch boxes for black ones with the word "Destroyer" on it. A lot of us dropped our G.I. Joe and Evel Knievel for a Gene Simmons action figure. There were posters and t-shirts everywhere with these guys on them and KISS became somewhat of an alliance of head bangers with obsessive compulsive disorder.

Honda came out with a KISS motorcycle. There were KISS Christmas tree ornaments. It was outrageous but the market flew like a 747.

All of these sights and sounds had a profound influence on millions of young people including a kid in Dallas named Darrell.

Darrell wanted to play lead guitar just like Ace Freely and before long he could play circles not only around Ace but practically anyone playing guitar in his genre. Millions of people heard Darrell's music though a band named "Pantara" and Darrell influenced little kids the same way Ace Freely had influenced him.

Last year when "Dimebag" Darrell Abbot was murdered on stage in Columbus it sent a cold chill into the hard rock world. By all accounts, the guitarist was a gentle and good guy that left a family and untold numbers of fans devastated at the loss.

For those of us that didn't know the music of the self proclaimed "Cowboys from Hell" the tragedy of his death and his unusual stage name caused us to turn our heads and wonder. A "dime bag" of course refers to ten dollars worth of dope and was part of the whole theme to the kind of lifestyle that the boys in KISS and Pantara loved to sing about.

From what I can find on the internet a "dime bag," these days, or $10 worth of weed is about 4.8 grams. Very important information if you're a jobless pothead waiting for an opportunity to go through your wife's purse.

While the tragedy and the violence of Dimebag's death is no laughing matter, I can't help but grin at Darrell's outlandish funeral. True to form, Dimebag was buried in a "KISS Kasket," a coffin completely covered with a specially laminated photomural that featured the KISS logo and images of all the band members. The words "KISS Forever" were imprinted on the side of the casket.

If you're thinking about getting yourself a KISS Kasket, there is no need to wait until your temperature drops. The marketing gurus at the KISS enterprise want you to know that the 'KISS Kasket' is water proof and can also be used as a beer cooler for you and your friends.

"This is the ultimate KISS collectible," said bassist Gene Simmons. "I love livin', but this makes the alternative look pretty da-- good." How profound for Gene to admit that KISS makes death look good.

So get yours now and party out of your burial box. It will only cost you $4700 and it comes autographed by all four band members.

See, in this world, when someone is extreme and excessive about something they are considered passionate and dedicated and that's the kind of press they get. I mean why wouldn't a head-banger like Dimebag Darrell be buried in a KISS Kasket? - - It was what his life was all about.

However, when a Christian dedicates his entire life to the Kingdom of God, he should not expect the same positive press. No matter how good of a guy he is, no matter how many millions of pounds of food he gives away to poor people, if he is high profile he will be labeled a right winged, evangelical, fundamentalist nut.

I know a lot of Christians are afraid of being too devout and devoted to Jesus and His cause because of what others might think. Not the Brewer! If you are going to be a Christian, at the very least you should be one that everybody else can tell is a Christian.

I know that someone out there is calling me a Bible thumpin', Jesus lovin', Pew jumpin', Red State, Hill Billy, Jesus Freak. I understand that and I have never one time needed a Melatonin to put me to sleep because my little tummy was upset that someone thinks that I am too dedicated to what I believe. They are supposed to think those things about me and besides that; I call my self those things!

Being called names is not that big of a deal anyway. See, KISS understood the principle that you do not influence the masses by being timid about what you believe. They shouted their dark gospel into what everyone else thought was inappropriate places and they won the hearts of millions by remaining true to who they are.

I wish the church of Jesus Christ had more people with that kind of zeal and passion for His righteous cause. What America needs is not a watered down, seeker friendly, self help, feel good message from timid and skittish believers.

Be bold with how God has changed your life! Be courageous in proclaiming the Word of God! Let Jesus Christ be your life and not just a sliver of it.

I recently discovered that I have an ancestor by the name of M. Robert Farrar. I was really excited to see him in my family's genealogy because his story is found in Fox's Book of Martyrs. He was someone that carried the gospel into an extreme category, so much so that Bloody Mary had him burned at the stake in 1555. My 14th great uncle told the crowd that if he kicked and screamed while being burnt alive to pay no attention to the doctrine he had preached. True to form, he died a death that glorified the Savior that had changed his life forever.

Now that is what I would call excessive compulsive behavior and it was exactly what England needed.

SOMETHING TO SIP ON:

Webster's definition of "RADICAL" is: Departing markedly from the usual or customary.

If there is anything that Christianity needs today, it is a strong revival of radicalism. May you and I be identified as Christians not satisfied with "the usual or customary," but people that want and live something completely different in Christ.

Romans 12:2
And be not conformed to this world: but be ye transformed by the renewing of your mind, that ye may prove what is that good, and acceptable, and perfect, will of God.

• The radical Christian is one who stands out from the world and is unlike the world.

• The radical Christian will "depart from the usual or customary."

• The radical Christian will have a different mind than the majority of the church.

• The radical Christian lives by the will of God and not by the status quo.

- The radical Christian is a world changer that makes a difference as opposed to the cultural Christians and "Creasters" (Christmas/ Easter Christians) that are otherwise ill-relevant to the Kingdom of God.

AVOIDING THE FREAK SHOW

A few years ago I took my kids to the local water theme park for a day of fun in the sun and water slides. It was a great day as most of our excursions are, except for one thing. While sitting next to the pool and sipping on a slurpee, my tranquil afternoon was deeply disturbed by a man that I would describe as living proof of the yeti climbing out of the water next to me. He had enough course hair on his back to braid into dreadlocks. I have never seen anything like it.

I wasn't sure if I should back away or run and beg Chewbacca for his autograph. It was an amazing site to behold. I watched in disbelief as the water beaded off of his fur, the way that it would a beaver. That was more than five years ago and I try not to think about it today, but sometimes I just can't help myself. When the image of that man comes into my mind, I begin to recite **Philippians 4:8 and 9**, *"What so ever things are pure……. think on these things"*

This is the very reason I wear a shirt when I go swimming. Not because of my body hair but because of the feared looks of repulsion and of the sound of crying children once my glory is revealed. When fully clothed, I am really not that bad looking, but I do know what it is like to be a walking freak show.

I have had the privilege of visiting Uganda, East Africa four times over the past 8 years, and it is very easy to draw a crowd. All I have to do is stand on the corner of any village anywhere. The reason? There are no white people, no fat people and no people with beards in Uganda, and I am all of those things. Every person there is better looking than me. Behold the oddity!

Just stand me up anywhere over there and we have a crowd control problem. It is a strange and humiliating experience, that I have had a lot of fun with it.

People are terrified these days of not looking the same as everybody else. Need a face lift or tummy tuck? We can do that quicker than ever these days. We can contour your body with liposuction and break out enough botox to permanently make your forehead look like a Norman Rockwall painting.

I want to scream out, "Get over your self!" So what if we don't fit into the proper perimeters of perfect people these days? What's real is that today, more than ever before, it is scary to be different.

The fact of the matter is that I don't want to be different but I am. I would rather just blend into what is acceptable by everybody but I can't. I have tried all my life to avoid the freak show and fit into every crowd imaginable, but it has just never worked out.

There has always been something different about me. It was that way before I became a Christian and then greatly multiplied after I became a Christian. It's a strange thing to admit that you don't really fit in anywhere in this world. I get along well and even succeed in all kinds of arenas, but I am always aware that I somehow don't belong.

It's the fact that you are different though, that makes people look at you. It is not how you blend in that attracts people, it is how you stand out as different that causes folks to turn their heads.

This past week was Open Door Ministries 10th Anniversary. A lot of people that love us came out in droves to support us and congratulate us.

When I got ready to give my once in a decade discourse I simply announced something that everybody associated with us already knows. We are different. We are a little bit off the wall. We don't really fit into the mainstream and that's okay. So we have slowly learned to embrace our own weirdness and after ten years, I believe it is God's plan.

If you are not a Christian and you feel like you don't fit in anywhere, I want to tell you that Jesus Christ is perfect for you. I want to encourage you and tell you that though people have rejected you, Jesus promises that He will not. He knows first hand what it means to be rejected and He will take you if you humble yourself and go to Him.

If you are a Christian, hear me on this, you don't have to look like everybody else in Christianity and talk like everybody else. Folks didn't go out to see John the Baptist because he looked and sounded like everybody else. They flocked to him because he was different. God is not going to hold you responsible for conforming to man; He will hold you responsible for submitting to Him!

If you are a Christian and plan on remaining real and genuine you are not going to fit into the cookie cutter mold that is traditionally accepted among the mainstream. That's okay. Be real anyway. Be passionate in your Christianity even if you don't fit into the norm. Stay in love with Jesus in spite of what others might say. It is Him that made you different and He likes you that way.

Jesus didn't fit into the perimeters of perfect looking people any better than you and I do, even though He really was perfect in every sense of the word.

Isaiah 53:2-3
He has no form or comeliness;
And when we see Him,
There is no beauty that we should desire Him.
He is despised and rejected by men,
A Man of sorrows and acquainted with grief.
And we hid, as it were, our faces from Him;
He was despised, and we did not esteem Him. (NKJV)

SOMETHING TO SIP ON:

I wonder if God thinks you are good looking or butt ugly. It doesn't have much to do with what's in the mirror, it all has to do with what's in your heart.

1Samuel 16:7
But the LORD said unto Samuel, Look not on his countenance,
or on the height of his stature; because I have refused him:
for the LORD seeth not as man seeth; for man looketh on the
outward appearance, but the LORD looketh on the heart.

WELL EARNED WAGES FOR MOM

So last week was Mother's day (2005) and I think it appropriate to continue in the spirit of appreciation to all the selfless moms out there. There are lots of famous moms in our culture and here are just a few to sip on while you enjoy this morning's cup.

There is Mother Goose, Old Mother Hubbard, Mother Land, Mother Earth, and Mother Russia. The later two points out that even socialist and communists can't help but love Mom.

There is 'Mother may I,' Mothers Against Drunk Driving and mother-in-law. Is it because of a lot of mothers-in-law that we have to have Mothers Against Drunk Driving, I wonder?

There is Ma Kettle, Ma Richards, Ma Barker, and Ma Bell. Mommy Dearest (yikes), Grand Ma Moses, Grandma cookies (one of my favorites), Granny Clampet, Mama Mia, Mama's Pizza and "Mama's Don't Let your Babies Grow Up to be Cowboys." Even Willie loves his mama.

You may also remember Mother Theresa or have spotted the Mother Ship in your back pasture. Maybe you are hoping for the Mother Load when you are scratching that ticket.

Before Saddam Hussein jumped into his spider hole to hide in the dirt he claimed to bring us the Mother of all wars.

Why do we love mom so much? I think because in a lot of ways she is a Marvel Comic super hero. Her sharp eyes can see everything from cruel sibling injustice to the sneaked cookies that you hid under the bed. Her incredible mental powers include the ability to know when you are telling a lie. She has legs that go the extra mile and hands that give lots of pats on the back. She has shoulders strong enough to bear the burdens of the entire house plus a purse that acts as a portable candy store, first aid station and the First National Bank.

Her feet have circled the globe at least once in search of keys, mittens and important papers and strode thousands of additional miles picking up toys. She knows where to find the kitchen utensils and that they are always in the dirt outside.

She is the greatest gerbil hunter in all the family. Her arms are just right for giving great big hugs, and her heart is made of gold. She's Mother--The female parent. Bottle warmer, diaper changer, nurse that makes room calls, family chauffer, family counselor, the cook, the maid, over worked and underpaid and the unsung hero of our day. You probably call her mom.

I could spend this whole article telling you about what an awesome mother I had growing up. There are not enough words in this whole paper to describe how selfless my mother was to me and my three siblings. She was not just mom to me but to all of my friends as well.

We played football, were on the rodeo team, and my brother was an all-star baseball player. We did drama, Webellos, Cub Scouts and Boy Scouts. We attended every dance and major function and even malfunction that school had to offer.

There was my mom acting like she was enjoying my poetry reading or listening to our very first country band when we were only sixth graders.

I was about fifteen years old before I discovered that not every mom cooked an awesome supper every night. She was able to do all of that and still go to nursing school, which was an education that would come in handy.

When my teenage friend got shot gun peppered in the back by an upset daddy for an unscheduled visitation to his daughter, it was my mom that doctored him.

When I hung my little brother by the neck for daring to sit on my favorite tree limb, it was Mom that resuscitated him.

When my brother set me on fire by lighting my aftershave it was Mother that took care of me.

When I dropped my baby sister out of the tree house it was my mother that stitched her up.

When my sister Missy got trampled by a horse in a back pasture stampede it was Mom that nursed her from that concussion.

She took care of us through snake bites, scarlet fever, spinal meningitis, car wrecks, broken bones, staff infections, braces, all manner of strange rashes in unspeakable places, surgeries and removed splinters, nails and BBs from our bodies. She loved me enough to hug me and loved me enough to beat the fire out of me when I needed it.

The Bible gives reference to the selfless mother of Moses in Exodus Chapter two. She protected her baby boy when it was seemingly impossible to do so and she did it as unto the Lord.

Because of her wisdom and her trust in God for her little bundle of joy, God saw to it that she saw her child grow into the full stature of a man. God also saw to it that she received wages from the local king for doing so.

The principle is that God promises to reward mothers for raising their children to be godly people. That reward doesn't just come when you step foot in heaven, it is something well earned in the land of the living.

The Mother of Moses got paid for raising her own child. She didn't get any credit for being an awesome mom, but she did get rewarded. That's the way it is for all selfless and godly mothers. They don't get the credit they so deserve by their peers, but the do get rewarded by the Heavenly Father.

There are lots of moms out there that I don't know about but there is one that I do. She is still taking care of people today as a nurse for Doctor Daly's office in Cleburne. Her name was Sharon Jackson and she was an awesome mom.

"...Her children arise and call her blessed."
Proverbs 31:28

SOMETHING TO SIP ON:

A three year old boy opened the birthday gift from his grandmother, he discovered a water pistol. He squealed with delight and headed for the nearest sink.

The three year olds mother was not so pleased and turned to her mother and said, "I'm surprised at you. Don't you remember how we used to drive you crazy with water guns?"

The grandmother smiled and then replied, "Yes, I do remember."

SPLENDID BEHAVIOR

Micah 6:6-8

With what shall I come before the LORD and bow down before the exalted God? Shall I come before him with burnt offerings, with calves a year old? Will the LORD be pleased with thousands of rams, with ten thousand rivers of oil? Shall I offer my firstborn for my transgression, the fruit of my body for the sin of my soul? He has showed you, O man, what is good. And what does the LORD require of you? To act justly and to love mercy and to walk humbly with your God.

I read an excellent article from Pastor Richard Burkley of Christ Lutheran Church in La Mesa, California. I thought I would pass part of it on in this week's cup of Jehovah Java. As you get ready to take your first sip, let me ask you a question -- what would you do in this situation?

Recently a man and his wife went to a restaurant that features steak and a salad bar. As they dined, a girl approached the salad bar with a 5-gallon bucket of Thousand Island dressing. Before she reached the salad bar she caught her heel and launched the 5-gallon container of dressing all over this one guy.

Imagine the scene: He has Thousand Island dressing from the top of his head to the bottom of his shoes; dripping off his forehead, off his chin, on the lapels of his suit, all over his tie, all over his pants, all over his shoes. He is a mess. Now if you were the one covered by Thousand Island dressing, what would you do? How would you respond?

This guy decides to go postal. He starts calling this poor girl every name a marine drill sergeant ever used. And he says, "I can't believe just how stupid you are. Look at this! This is the first chance I've had to wear this suit. It cost me $350 and you have completely ruined it."

She's saying, "Sir..." and she's trying to clean it up.

"Get away from me! You caused enough damage already." His wife chimes in. "That's right. It's a $350 suit...blah ... blah ... blah."

Everybody in the whole restaurant is watching, and he demands, "I want to see the manager." The manager comes out and says, "Is there a problem?" "Yes there's a problem. This stupid girl has ruined my suit. It's the first chance I've had to wear it. It costs $350."

"Sir, we'll clean your suit for you. No problem. We'll take care of that." The guy says, "I don't want my suit cleaned. I want a new suit. It's completely ruined. I want a new suit. I want a check right now for $350." The manager disappeared, the guy with him. I imagine he wrote him a check and justice was served.

Now what is interesting about this story is that this happened on a Sunday afternoon. So why in the world would a guy be in a suit on a Sunday afternoon? Oh, I don't know. Probably just came from hearing a great sermon on loving your neighbor as yourself or about turning the other cheek.

People who work in the food service industry will tell you that the very worst people to wait on are the people who just got out of church on a Sunday morning. That's tragic, because, friends, we're called to worship not only inside the walls of a church, but to worship without walls. We are not called to go to church we are called to be the church!

We're called to be Jesus in restaurants even with Thousand Island all over us. I would say that we are called to act like Jesus especially if Thousand Island is all over us.

That Big Dummy had an opportunity to reach that entire restaurant with an example of God's love and an encouraging word, in Jesus' name, to the freaked out waitress. Instead He gave people an excellent excuse for why they don't want to go to church.

The way we respond to the mess in our lives will either bear good or bad fruit. I think that there are probably two reasons why people are not living for Jesus Christ. One reason is because they have never met a Christian and then the second reason is because they have met one.

In the late 1800s, there lived a famous black Cowboy by the name of Bose Ikard. He worked for Charles Goodnight, the prominent Texas rancher and developer of the Goodnight –Loving Cattle Trail from Belknap, Texas, to Fort Sumner, New Mexico.

A close friendship developed between Bose Ikard and Goodnight who trusted his friend "farther than any living man." Goodnight said, "He was my detective, banker, and everything else in Colorado, New Mexico, and the other wild country I was in."

When Ikard died, Goodnight honored him with a granite marker in Weatherford, Texas, where he was buried. The epitaph reads:

"Bose Ikard served with me four years on the Goodnight-Loving Trail, never shirked a duty or disobeyed an order, rode with me in many stampedes, participated in three engagements with Comanche's, splendid behavior."

I pray that we as Christians will have the same thing said about us when it comes time for our stone to be chiseled. God help us to be more like Bose Ikard and may it be written, "Splendid behavior."

SOMETHING TO SIP ON:

Who keeps his temper, calm and cool,
    Will find his wits in season;
But rage is weak, a foaming fool,
    With neither strength nor reason.
And if a thing be hard to bear
    When nerve and brain are steady,
If fiery passions rave and tear,
    It finds us maimed already.

Who yields to anger conquered lies—
    A captive none can pity;
Who rules his spirit, greater is
    Than he who takes a city.

From "Keep your Temper"
By Ellen P. Allerton

Walls of Corn and Other Poems
Ellen P. Allerton
(Hiawatha, KS: Harrington Printing Company. 1894)
Pages 56-57

FINAL EXAM

It's final exam time for our high school and college students and those of higher learning. We are talking about burning the proverbial midnight oil with late night, stressed out, studies full of coffee and red bull energy drinks. This is when the fear of failure tends to make a young person "downsize" from being bullet proof to a mere weak mortal once again.

There are two kinds of tests that send terror into the hearts of every unprepared high school student. One is a surprise pop quiz. This is a powerful and time tested tool in the teacher's arsenal against ignorance. The other is the final exam that you do know is coming and can't be escaped.

Some people do not have to be tested for the rest of us to know that their brain gets a lot less mileage than most. For example, let me tell you about Ramon Westmiller.

Ramon had a terrible accident at work, so he filled out an insurance claim. The insurance company contacted him and asked for more information. This was his response:

"You said in your letter that I should explain more fully, the circumstances of my accident. I trust the following details will be sufficient.

"I am an amateur radio operator and I was working alone on the top section of my new 80-foot tower. When I had completed my work, I discovered that I had, over the course of several trips up the tower, brought up about 300 pounds of tools and spare parts. Rather than carry the tools and material down by hand, I decided to lower the items down in a small barrel by using the pulley attached to a pole at the top of the tower. Securing the rope at ground level, I went to the top of the tower and loaded the tools and parts into the barrel. Then I went back to the ground and untied the rope, wrapped it tightly around my wrists to ensure a slow decent of the tools."

"You will note from my medical records that I weigh only 155 pounds. Due to the larger weight of the tools I was jerked off the ground. I could not let go of the rope. Needless to say, I went quickly up the side of the tower. At about the 40-foot level, I met the barrel coming down. This explains my fractured skull and broken collarbone. But this only slowed my ascent slightly. I continued my rapid ascent, not stopping until the fingers of my right hand were jammed deep into the pulley at the top. I still could not get free of the rope but as the barrel of tools hit the ground, the bottom fell out of the barrel."

"Now the weight of the tools was absent and the empty barrel now weighed only about 20 pounds. As you might imagine, I began a rapid descent down the side of the tower. In the vicinity of the 40-foot level, once again, I met the barrel coming up. This accounts for the two fractured ankles, and the lacerations of my legs and lower body. The encounter with the barrel slowed me enough to lessen my injuries when I fell onto the pile of tools and, fortunately, only three vertebrae were cracked. I am sorry to report, however, that as I lay there on the tools, in pain, unable to stand and watching the empty barrel 80 feet above me, I was finally able to get free from the rope, but unable to move quickly enough to get out of the way of the barrel as it fell."

This brother is in need of some serious adult supervision.

Or maybe you have heard about the 33 year old Truck Driver named Larry Walters. He's the guy that back in 1983 tied 45 weather balloons full of helium to a rigged up lawn chair and took a 45 minute ride to 16,000 feet before he got cold, shot some balloons with a BB gun and crashed into a power line.

In spite of himself, he was uninjured in the crash. The FAA (Federal Aviation Administration) was not amused though. Regional safety inspector Neal Savoy said the flying lawn chair was spotted by TWA and Delta jetliner pilots at 16,000 feet.

No exam needed here.

Now let me get a little bit serious with you. When a teacher tells you what is going to be on your final exam and when you fail that final exam do not expect the teacher to have mercy on you, because it is an insult to that teacher. When they have gone to all the trouble to tell you exactly what would be on the test there is no excuse for you to not know it.

2000 years ago Jesus Christ gave his disciples a "Pop Quiz" that would become everyone's final exam. He went to a lot of trouble to let us know exactly what would be our true final exam and we had best pay attention to it. The text is found in **Matthew 16:13-16** and it reads like this.

When Jesus came into the coasts of Caesarea Philippi, he asked his disciples, saying, Whom do men say that I the Son of man am? And they said, Some say that thou art John the Baptist: some, Elias; and others, Jeremiah, or one of the prophets. He saith unto them, But whom say ye that I am? And Simon Peter answered and said, Thou art the Christ, the Son of the living God.

Study the material if you want, but I am getting to know the teacher. I learned a long time ago that knowing the teacher giving the exam is the key to passing every exam. Pay attention to this, knowing the teacher **IS** the exam when it comes to eternity.

Pop Quiz, kids. **Who do you say Jesus is?**

PERSISTENCE PAYS

Last week I took my father-in-law on a quick trip to East Texas. Though Ray acts a lot older than he is; he is as good as gold and we get along really well. However sometimes he can rattle on and deliberately try to peg a person's "cringe meter" just to get a response and he doesn't really care what that response is. For him it's a form of cheap entertainment but for me it meant that the three hour drive would seem more like a NASA assignment to Mars.

As I began to openly pray for a deer to run out in front of me he commenced to enlighten me in a long joyful yarn and in no uncertain terms, how-the-world turned, on various and sundry subjects. His feelings on his wife (of nearly 45 years) based on the fact were that her side of the family was of Scottish descent called the Macdade's. His description of the Macdade clan was that they were "the most *stubbornnessed* people that ever lived." I am not sure if "*stubbornessed*" is a real word but for him it was a perfect portrayal.

Never mind the fact that if his wife were Catholic, she would have already been canonized and folks would be visiting her statue in Rome. The woman is a saint in the truest since of the word.

So I tried to defend her like any good son-in-law would, by saying, "Excuse me, but I think that if there is anybody that might fall into the most stubborn category it would certainly be you." He looked at me with total clarity and it was then that I realized the whole thing was a setup.

He said, "No Troy you are wrong. I'm not stubborn, I'm determined and there is a big difference."

My father-in-law is really funny in an old codger kind of way and there is something to be said about being determined and full of unwavering resolution. The bottom line is that persistence pays. His comment got me to thinking about the importance of overcoming and holding on when others fall out.

In the book of Revelation the promises that Jesus gives to the church are not just for folks that believe, they are for folks that overcome. Seven different times does Jesus promise awesome things to "He that overcometh." **(Rev 2:7, 2:11, 2:17, 2:26, 3:5, 3:12 & 3:21)**

Revelation 21:7 says *He that overcometh shall inherit all things; and I will be his God, and he shall be my son.* (KJV)

I want to encourage you to be more like the Macdade clan and the Ray Knight family of Azle. Dare to be an over comer. Keep fighting the good fight. Don't fall out because others around you are.

President Calvin Coolidge said, "Nothing in the world can take the place of persistence. Talent will not; nothing is more common than unsuccessful men with talent. Genius will not; unrewarded genius is almost a proverb. Education will not; the world is full of educated derelicts. Persistence and determination alone are omnipotent."

Great people are often just ordinary people with extraordinary determination. They are leather bent and stubborn. They simply won't quit.

A person's character and influence is not determined by his fame, his position, his wealth or even his station in life; but rather what it takes to discourage that person. You can learn much about a person as they respond to criticism or failure.

What does it take to discourage you? -- Someone's disapproval? Unplanned obstacles? Unmet expectations? It might even be success. A lot of people shut down and quit after achieving small goals and they fail to go forward. Don't do that! Keep going. Don't stop. Keep advancing in Christ.

Paul writes in **Galatians 6.9**, *"So let's not allow ourselves to get fatigued doing good. At the right time we will harvest a good crop if we don't give up, or quit."* (The Message)

SOMETHING TO SIP ON:

A lady named Beth Anne DeCiantis attempted to qualify for the 1992 Olympic Trials Marathon. According to the rules, a female runner must complete the 26 mile, 385 yard race in less than two hours, forty five minutes to compete at the Trials.

Beth started strong but began having trouble around mile 23. She reached the final straight-away at 2:43, with just two minutes left to qualify. Two hundred yards from the finish, she stumbled and fell. Dazed, she stayed down for 20 seconds. The crowd yelled, "Get up! Get up!" The clock was ticking - 2:44, less than a minute to go. Beth Anne staggered to her feet and began walking. Five yards short of the finish, with ten seconds to go, she fell again. She began to crawl, the crowd cheering her on, and she crossed the finish line on her hands and knees. Her time? Two hours, 44 minutes, 57 seconds.

She only made it by 3 seconds, but she was as in as the first person to cross the finish line. Just like that, if you give up 3 seconds too soon, you miss the mark just as far as the person that never competed. If you miss the train by 3 seconds you still miss the train. Don't give up.

Hebrews 12:1 reminds us to run our race with perseverance and never give up!

Despite what you are facing this week, hang in there. Don't get discouraged, don't' give up! Stay the course! Jesus will never leave you or forsake you. The prize He has set before you is worth whatever you are going through.

He has never given up on you and He never will because He really understands that persistence pays.

SORRY, WRONG NUMBER

In a few weeks all of our cell phone numbers are being released to telemarketing companies and we will all start receiving those beloved sales calls on our mobile phones. Isn't that great? I can hardly wait. I look forward to this kind of event the way I look forward to my doctor's visit after my 40th birthday.

Look, I know that a lot of good people work these kinds of jobs and that it's a hard job to have but it is just so easy to hate the entire industry. As a pastor, my phone rings a lot and in between those very important phone calls have been plenty of attempts to sell me siding. It puts you in a bad position because you don't want to be rude, yet you don't want another set of storm windows. What's a nice guy supposed to do?

Thankfully, America has been introduced to the National Do Not Call List. It is a number you can call from the phone that you don't want rang by a telemarketer. You and your wireless peers should pay attention to this. Once you call the number (888-382-1222) you are listed for 5 years; the idea is that telemarketers are not allowed to call anymore. It is a very polite way of saying, "please don't call me for at least the next five years." I like that.

Others have been famous for using less than polite tactics to stop their dinners from being interrupted. Sometime back, a reporter for the Miami Harold exacted terrible vengeance on the American Telemarketing Association (ATA) by printing their phone number for complainers to call. So many people did call that number that the executive director of the ATA, Tim Searcy issued a statement to the press.

"The ATA received no warning about the article from Barry or anyone connected with him," Searcy complained that, "the Barry column has had harmful consequences for the ATA. An ATA staffer has spent about five hours a day for the past six days monitoring the voice mail and clearing out messages."

Can you imagine? The ATA complained that it received NO WARNING that it was going to get unwanted calls. Not only that, but these unwanted calls were an INCONVENIENCE, and WASTED THE ATA'S TIME. Wow! That's how I define ironic.

You know there are some calls you do and some you do not want to take. The Bible gives us clear warning of a call that all of us have got to hear whether it is convenient or not.

Proverbs 21:13
Whoso stoppeth his ears at the cry of the poor,
he also shall cry himself, but shall not be heard.

SOMETHING TO SIP ON:

According to the Census Bureau, Johnson County (THE AREA WHERE I LIVE) has 139,068 citizens. Out of that, 18.8% are below the poverty level or over the age of 65. That means that there are a lot of people around us that need our help and that is a call that we have got to answer.

This of course is no surprise to those of us that reach out to the poor of our area. In a good year Open Door Ministries will give away more than 300,000 pounds of food to those around us and we by no means have cornered the market on making a difference.

There are a lot of ministries and just good people that will answer that call when they get it. I hope that you will do the same this year.

I just got back from visiting orphanages in Uganda last Saturday, but let me tell you that you don't have to travel 10,000 miles to hear the poor cry out.

In 2005 Open Door Ministries gave away right at 1,000,000 pounds of food to our local poor and several million pounds of clothing, health care items and paper goods. When you support Open Door Ministries you are directly helping poor families; families that you otherwise would never have had contact with nor would you have touched their lives.

Let the Lord Jesus Christ give you a heart for the poor and make a difference by getting involved in somebody else's world. If *you will*, then God promises that *He will* help you in your times of trouble. (See **Psalms 41**)

This is one inconvenient call that is in all our best interests to answer.

GET IT TOGETHER

I am not an evolutionist in any sense of the term but I might be a good example for one.

Folks that have an agenda to run God out of His universe will point to the remnant of "leg" bones in a whale. They will say, "See, this thing used to have legs." Or they will point to a chromosome of the great ape and show us how we've got the same stuff in our makings.

Well I am here to announce that I've got great news for all evolutionists. Anyone looking for the connection of human-ape ancestry need not look any further than me. You see, like the chimpanzee, I can not hold a hammer.

If you see me holding a hammer it is either because I am trying to look cool or because I am using it to defend myself against some perceived threat. Such threats as my much hated squirrels, "tree rats" as I like to call them that taunt me in my own back yard. Oh their funny but I can't help but throw a hammer at them every now and then.

My ability to build anything or actually hit a nail with a hammer ranks right up there with my ability to actually hit a squirrel with a metal object. There are just some things that, no matter how hard you try, you can't do it. Contorting my body like an Olympic gymnast is a clear impossibility for me and being a real handyman around the house is another.

For those of us are mechanically challenged, we have learned the value of duct tape and super glue. I reach for these items the way my grandfather reaches for the Campho-Phenique. Don't let my Granddad doctor you unless you want to smell like his little green bottle of snake oil and don't ask me to repair anything unless you find wide, metallic tape attractive and fitting to your décor. Duct tape might be ugly but it holds things together, and there are a lot of things that we need to hold together these days.

Way back on November the 15th of 1963, a preacher by the name of William Branham preached a message in New York City called "The World is Falling Apart." That was a good title for a message in those days because sixty-three is the year that we took prayer out of school and the Beatles invaded America changing our teenage culture forever. It was the year we entered the Vietnam War.

Just seven days after he preached his message, America would watch the First Lady climb onto the back of a limo, speeding through downtown Dallas as we began to mourn the death of our President.

I wonder what the preachers of the sixties would think of the day we live in now. I think instead of the common, seeker friendly, three-point self help messages we so often hear, there would be a whole lot more sermons titled "The World is Falling Apart."

In this weeks column from a caffeinated Christian I want to encourage you to wake up and smell the coffee! There are some things that you've got to get together and if you don't get a handle on it quick, it really will fall apart.

Our marriages, our finances, our relationships with our kids, our very sanity had better be held together by something much stronger than us. In the book that Paul wrote to the Colossians, the Bible gives us a "heads up" on something much stronger than super glue.

In speaking of Jesus, he says the following:

> *For by him were all things created, that are in heaven,*
> *and that are in earth, visible and invisible,*
> *whether they be thrones, or dominions, or principalities,*
> *or powers: all things were created by him, and for him:*
> *And he is before all things, and by him all things consist.*
> ***Colossians 1:16-17***

When the Bible says that by Jesus "all things consist," it literally means that by Him all things are "held together." That's good news for those of us not skilled at holding things together.

If you will let Him, Jesus can hold you and your life together in a way like no one else can. As the Bible says, He is the creator of the systems that do hold things together, from the gravitational force of the largest solar system to the electrical force that holds together the tiniest atom. He knows how to embrace things in a way that they can not fall apart.

I encourage you to not reject the Lord's embrace. If you will get real with Him, He will get real with you. He wants to hold you close without letting go. He doesn't want your heart and your head scattered throughout your brief life time nor does he want your family and your house divided and headed in different directions.

Call on Him and let Him do His work.

He can fix things so much better than the rest of us can and He doesn't need duct tape or super glue to do it. After all, Jesus is a carpenter.

SOMETHING TO SIP ON:

Anytime anybody has wanted to get close to somebody, there has always been one thing that works. You go out to eat.

If it's a hot date, you go to a fancy restaurant.

If it's an old friend you go to the pub or to your favorite hot dog stand.

If it's a family reunion you all sit down at the table together.

That's what human beings do when you want to be close to somebody.

Something I have observed about Jesus is that, after His resurrection, He didn't gather everyone together for a formal church service. Over and over again He gathered the disciples to sit down and eat together. They ate in the house, on the beach, and the promise again of what will happen in heaven at the "marriage supper of the Lamb."

In Luke Chapter 24 when the resurrected Jesus appeared before the disciples, His friends were more than just a little freaked out. Jesus spoke peace to them and they still didn't know what to think. Jesus showed them His scars and they still didn't know what to think. Then Jesus asked them a strange question. "You got anything to eat?" It was only after this, the disciples were able to really get excited about this being Jesus in the room.

This had to be Jesus, not because He walked through a wall; not because He had nail scars, but they knew it was Him and that He was for real when He wanted to eat with them. That was the Jesus they knew and understood.

Luke 24:41
And while they yet believed not for joy, and wondered, he said unto them, Have ye here any meat?
And they gave him a piece of a broiled fish,
and of a honeycomb.
And he took it, and did eat before them.

Jesus Christ is nothing like traditional Christianity has portrayed Him. He's not after our talent, our money, or our church attendance alone. He is after our fellowship. Look closely at what Jesus says to the church in **Revelation 3:20** and see how He wants to be close to us.

Behold, I stand at the door, and knock:
if any man hear my voice, and open the door,
I will come in to him, and will sup with him, and he with me.
Rev 3:20

CRAZY THANKFULNESS

A few years back, a small town disc jockey narrowly missed being on the plane that killed Buddy Holly; and then broke out into the country music scene with his own brand of Outlaw Music. Waylon Jennings was his name and besides having a famous voice, he had the most famous hands in the world for a time. It was his hands that were seen on the weekly introduction to the Dukes of Hazard.

In one of the songs that made him famous, Waylon proclaimed, "I've always been crazy but it's helped me from going insane."

It seems that singers love to sing about craziness in general. No matter what kind of music you have been into throughout the years, chances are, there is a "Crazy" song that fits your radio station.

One of the most famous crazy songs is actually called "Crazy" and was written by another outlaw named Willie Nelson and sung by Patsy Cline. I can remember Crazy Arms by Ray Price, Crazy Train by Ozzie Ozbourne and Crazy World by the Scorpions. Queen came out with a song called Stone Cold Crazy and latter a band named Metallica recorded the same tune.

At about the same timeframe, a European group called "Fine Young Cannibals" had a hit titled "She Drives me Crazy." I remember John Cougar singing "I need a lover that won't drive me crazy." Much more recent crazy hits include "Crazy Nights" by Lonestar and yet another song called "Crazy" by Britney Spears. I went to the web and looked up the word "Crazy' in various song lists and it became very apparent music publishers know that craziness sales big in the music industry.

Other artists with songs titled "Crazy" include; Usher, Aerosmith, Tori Amos, TLC, Supertramp, Cat Stevens, IMX, Pat Benatar, Barenaked Ladies, Abba and Weird Al Yancovic.

Let me do like the band called Heart did and go crazy on you for just a minute.

This is a crazy day in which we live. It's extreme, outrageous and full of useless information that can quickly derail you from knowing the truth and divert your attention from what you need to be thinking about – to well, think about crazy things.

When a police officer gets ready to go to work, he does so with body armor in the form of a bullet proof vest. In taking the times serious he knows it's dangerous out there. Just like that, the Bible promises the helmet of salvation for God's people and for those of us that believe these are dangerous times, we had better armor up.

There are more things to drive you crazy today than in any other day before us.-Every new CNN top of the hour news show increases your worry list. The demands on you are incredible, and faster than ever, stress and nervous tension can wrap itself around your head the way the alien did John Hurt.

I want to give you a biblical solution from going crazy in a day when it is so easy to slip over the edge. It's a word that we do not use very much but it and the other forms of this word are found no less than three hundred times throughout the scriptures.

The word I am talking about is *thankfulness* and it really is an antidote to going postal.

In Paul's masterpiece of theology to the Romans there is a scripture in the first chapter spelling out the point I am trying to make.

Romans 1:21
Because that, when they knew God, they glorified him not as God, neither were thankful; but became vain in their imaginations, and their foolish heart was darkened.

Paul says here, people who refuse to glorify God are joined at the hip to people who refuse to be thankful. After that, he gives the natural progression of an unthankful heart and the Kings James boys say they "became vain in their imaginations."

To have vanity in your thoughts means to think on things that, simply do not matter. When your mind slips away from purposely being thankful, it defaults to subjects of no substance and you end up thinking about things you should not or as the Bible puts it, "v*ain imaginations.*"

In short, refusing to be thankful will make you crazy and without even knowing it you will drive everybody around you crazy as well. It really has nothing to do with your circumstances, but being thankful is a disciplined condition of the heart. You have to do it on purpose. God doesn't ask us to be thankful <u>for</u> everything, He commands us to be thankful <u>in</u> everything.

God doesn't want our minds running off down an endless list of rabbit trails and hurtful scenarios so He commands us to be thankful. By ordering us to give thanks, God is saying that we should give Him glory and quit being "crazy." While that might be a tall order, if you think about that, it's really not asking too much.

SOMETHING TO SIP ON:

Thanksgiving is a time for feasting yes, but let us not forget to actually give thanks. I am not talking about a ritualistic prayer, but a sober assessment, being thankful for all that we have. If we can get past us, I mean our hurts and our problems and disappointments, we might become temporarily sane enough to see how blessed we really are.

Do you have a list of things you are thankful for or has your foolish heart been darkened? It's not a put down, it's just what happens to all of us if we fail to stop and truly give thanks.

THE DAY AFTER

Back in the eighties there was a popular television show that captivated the imagination of Americans called "The Day After." It was a show about nuclear holocaust and the terrible aftermath of trying to live in a United States that glowed in the dark.

I associate chaos, confusion and panic with the day after, but not the day after an invasion or a bombing. I am talking about the day after Thanksgiving. The Friday that always follows Thanksgiving is a dark day to the Brewer household. It's the day when crazy people travel across our roads and head to the malls. It's the day when Christmas buying begins and every one's car potentially becomes a weapon or an object of great disrespect towards other people.

I must confess to you I could never have a 'Honk if you love Jesus" bumper sticker. The main reason being I have a tendency to suffer extreme bouts of road rage if anyone honks at me for any reason. I am a Christian, but I am also a Texan and my immediate involuntary reaction to someone honking at me tends to be the same as someone slapping my wife or a home invasion. I take it very personally and could loose my testimony as quick as a duck jumps on a June bug.

I know that in other states people honk at each other all the time but I don't want to live in those places. We Texans tend to take rude behavior very seriously. "Yes, keep honking, I need time to reload!"

I am convinced that the most dangerous place in the entire world, with no disrespect to our troops, is not the Arabian Desert; but is in fact your local Wal-Mart parking lot. Anything can happen with morale so low and frustrations so high. How can you not be frustrated in that terrible place?

You spend an hour of your life waiting in line for some poor teenager to frantically work the counter while most of the other cash registers are empty. What you thought was about $35 worth of merchandise ended up being way over a hundred and fifty bucks because you kept finding stuff on sale and you were brought up to believe that a sale means you save money. Rubbish! Wal-Mart is proof that sales are from the devil.

You know how supermarkets put all of the individual candy items by the register where kids have to stand in line and at three feet from the ground? In the same way, all of Wal-Mart is designed for otherwise mature adults to grab things they really don't need and buy things they otherwise never would. You know it, yet you buy it.

There is the added frustration of dealing with what I call that "Wal-Mart feeling." It's the same sickening sensation I felt when I had scarlet fever as a child. It jumps on me the moment I get blasted by the cold air going through the front doors and it stays with me until long after I am gone. Without fail, after any visit to Wal-Mart I need decompression time. It takes at least an hour of mindless vegetation in front of the television to cure me of the terrible "Wal-Mart feeling."

But you add all of that mess to the day after Thanksgiving sale and what you have is a guaranteed outcome of mayhem in the parking lot.

A profound sense of terrible sarcasm comes over me. I fantasize of printing my own bumper stickers and slapping them onto cars I deem worthy.

"Caution: I brake for hallucinations."
"Don't take my signals literally."
"Warning: I swerve and hit people at random."
"Cover me I'm changing lanes."
"Now that you are kissing my bumper, do you wanna get married?"
"Honk if the twins fall out!"
"If you can read this, my trailer came loose."
"I took an IQ test and the results were negative."
"I support public aggravation."

And then sanity will slowly come back to me the way an old television used to warm up; instead of wanting to curse everybody I go back to wanting to bless folks again. Through clinched teeth maybe, but a blessing I will be.

Lord Jesus, help us not to loose our minds in the midst of the madness that is our culture in these last crazy days.

There is an incredible promise of God that comes to mind in times like these and you can find it in the book of Exodus.

And He said, My presence shall go with thee,
and I will give thee rest.
Exodus 33:14

This promise was not just for Moses 3500 years ago, but it is also for those of us that love the Lord today. He says we can have His presence and if we can have His presence, we can have His rest.

Jesus later would promise that He would be with us always even unto the ends of the world. I also like to say Jesus will be with us always even unto the ends of our rope.

You might be facing the Holidays and going through places where angles fear to tread, but make no mistake, Christ is not stressing out at your road map. In fact, He is the one that wrote your map. He really and truly will be with you, if you will let Him be God in your life. The promise He gives is His rest in all your goings and that even applies to shopping centers and malls.

SOMETHING TO SIP ON:

For those of us that are Christian, we have the promise that His presence is literally with us because He is literally living within us.

Colossians 1:27
To whom God would make known what [is] the riches of the glory of this mystery among the Gentiles; which is Christ in you, the hope of glory:

PAULA'S TRIBUTE
(Things that matter)

Many of you already know that my long time friend and personal secretary, Paula Ledbetter, died in her sleep last Friday morning. She was only 37 years old but she made 100 years worth of difference in our lives and in the world she lived in. Today's sip from the carpenter's cup is mixed with a bitter sweet tear or two. I hope you'll continue sipping as I honor my friend and glorify the Lord.

If you have ever been to one of our food outreaches, church services or music concerts, you have seen Paula. It has been the habit of my wife and me, not to go very far without her because she helped us to do everything. She cleaned the church, answered the phones, cut every ones hair for free, organized our big events, structured the deacons ministry, took food to folks that couldn't come to get it, arranged all of my evangelical meetings, helped me keep track of my newspaper columns, watched our kids, made me coffee and worked hard on all our missions trips.

I am convinced that if you look up the words *dedicated, selfless,* or maybe even *loyal* in the dictionary, you will see Paula's smiling face right beside it. We will miss her in such an incredible way because she made such a big difference in so many arenas.

Paula was an outstanding wife to her wonderful husband, John Ledbetter. She was a joy for John to come home to and their 18 year marriage was abundantly blessed. She selflessly served the love of her life in every way she could, especially in prayer and service. She stood by John and for John in all she did every day of the week.

Paula's skill as a mother was incredibly evident through the lives of her three teenage boys. All of them are fine young men with a strong balance of fun nature and hard dedication when they have to have it. She was a super-hero mom to her kids and I know that those boys will marry fine women someday because they have seen the perfect model of a wife and mother.

Paula was a joy to have as a daughter-in-law to Charlie and Jerri Ledbetter. She was a faithful friend to my wife and a devoted church secretary to Open Door.

If you missed Paula's funeral service, you missed one of the greatest send offs I have ever had the privilege of leading. Over 600 people tried to cram into a room that only held 250 and we literally applauded Paula's life and the Lord she loved so much.

It was easy to mark the qualities that made Paula so special. It was effortless to put together a sermon that praised God and honored Paula because she lived such an honorable life. It was simple to point out what a difference she made when you have hundreds of people packed in a room and hundreds more outside that can't get in -- because they all loved Paula so much.

I am telling you that God moved in such a powerful way at her funeral I almost got saved again myself! In all seriousness, from what I have been able to gather, 17 people dedicated their hearts to the Lord that day. It was an overwhelming moment of victory in a time when most are completely defeated.

That was true to form for Paula. She was always making something wonderful out of something bad. Whether it was a gourmet meal out of macaroni and leftovers or somebody's nasty feet in a pedicure, she knew how to turn bad things into good things.

This is the mark of people that truly follow Jesus Christ. Where there is darkness there is light. Where there is failure there is hope. Where there is pain there is healing. And finally where there is death there is victory.

In Luke 4:16 Jesus said; *"The Spirit of the Lord is on me, because he has anointed me to preach good news to the poor, to bind up the brokenhearted, to comfort all who mourn, and provide for those who grieve, to bestow on them a crown of beauty instead of ashes, the oil of gladness instead of a spirit of despair."*

We are all heartbroken at the death of our sister but by no means are we defeated. I mean, Paula was not defeated so why should we be? The fact of the matter is -- Paula's story doesn't end there and I thank God it doesn't. It may be a fact that Paula lost a long time battle last Friday but I know it's the truth that she did not loose the war. She has victory against death and it was won for her on a battle field 2000 years ago by a champion named Jesus Christ.

I wonder if I could stand at your funeral and declare certain victory for you the same way I did for Paula.

I wonder if I could stand and speak of your unwavering faith, your selfless service and your dedication to the things that really matter.

Or I wonder if your funeral would be a sad, boring sermon where the best thing I could say for you is that you liked to play golf or you had joined the union at work or maybe loved your dog or your cat.

The truth is that if your life is all about you and how you can advance your own personal agenda, the world will not be worse off without you. However, if you have the same testimony that Paula has, and you have spent your life serving God and serving those around you, we will always have good reason to celebrate your life and to truly mourn your death.

It is when you consider how short life really is, that you begin to get in a hurry to take care of the things that really do matter.

Teach us, oh Lord, to number our days that we may apply our hearts unto wisdom.
Psalms 90:12

I am proud of you Paula and I will see you on the great day!

SOMETHING TO SIP ON:

Just before Paula died I left for Costa Rica for a ten day mission's trip. I sent the column to her and asked her to send it to the newspaper for the Friday dead line and of course she was happy to do it.

On Thursday I had an eight hour lay over in Miami and I called the office to chat and slay some boredom.

Paula, who was not an overly affectionate, lovey-dovey person, said that she was glad I had called because she needed to read something to me.

She said that she had been thinking about the "Crazy Thankfulness" column and that God had prompted her to write down all the things she was thankful for in her relationship with my wife and me.

At first, I thought she was kidding because we always give each other such a hard time but when I made a joke she said "No for real, Troy, God told me to do this and I don't want you and Leanna to think that I take ya'll for granted."

For the next few minutes I listened while Paula went down a very long list of things she was thankful to the Lord for, in how Leanna and I had impacted her life and her family.

She gave us credit for a lot of things we didn't deserve and for quite some time she poured out her heart. She ended it by saying, "I have had good friends in my life but nobody has helped me be a friend to Jesus like you two have. I really thank God and love you with all my heart."

Afterward, there was a pause and I said, "Wow. I don't know what to say. Thank you Paula, I love you too. I'm also very thankful that God has hooked us up together and you and John are a huge blessing to us."

She was a little embarrassed about the whole thing and said "well, it was important to me that I told you that today."

When I hung up the phone I had no idea that Paula would go to sleep that night and wake up in heaven the next morning. I surely didn't think it would be our last conversation but I do remember hanging up and thinking, that was a little out of character for Paula to do that and I wondered what God was up to.

When Leanna called me the next day to tell me what had happened, it took a few minutes for me to have rational thought. As soon as I was able, I remembered our last conversation and then I knew what God was up to.

Thank you Jesus for setting me up for victory, as you have, all of those that loved Paula's selfless life.

Even in hard places I continue to find out how far out of the way Jesus will go to let us know He is with us and in perfect control.

God is so good and His promise is in that conversation I had with her in the Miami airport. It will not be our last conversation. We will have all eternity to verbally glorify the Lord.

A REVIEW OF JARHEAD

I don't think you will ever see Roger Ebert and Troy Brewer on the same TV show talking about the latest at the theater. Although the new wide screens might accommodate us, nobody wants to watch two fat guys jawing at the same time.

Movies are a huge part of our culture and I see a lot of them. I like movies and I like different kinds of movies. As a Christian I have decided there are certain lines I don't cross so there are tickets I will never buy but that doesn't mean I ban the medium altogether.

A movie can be cutting edge without being vulgar, like "Lord of the Rings." It can have strong and scary content without being explicit like "The Missing." It can have professional cops and shootouts without being full of offensive language as in "The fugitive." It can even have a high body count with out being improper and still be a good movie like they managed in "Tombstone" and "We Were Soldiers."

I am a Christian in a secular world and culture, and I understand that when I go to the movies I am not in a Christian arena.

However, you don t have to be a Christian to have a brain or to be decent.

Sometimes I will come across a movie that is so offensive it makes me want to gather other angry peasants with pitch forks to burn the Hollywood castle down. This happened to me last week.

I made one of the worst mistakes of my young life last Friday night and spent eight hard earned dollars on what I thought was going to be a pro-marine war movie called "JARHEAD." It should have been called "Jar-Jar binks" or maybe "Knucklehead!"

I had seen the trailers with Jamie Fox and it came complete with burning desert scenes and a short speech that ended with a "hoo-ah." I was ready to raise the flag.

What I did not know is that the godless, Americana haters that made this optical septic tank, could not be honest about the movie they had made, so they portrayed it in another light to get my eight dollars. Had it not been deceitfully advertised and it been honest to the actual content, the trailer would have sounded something like this - - -

Come see a movie that will grieve your spirit and make you want to take a shower afterwards. Be entertained with the forever use of the F-word and the mythical idea that there is no such thing as a professional American soldier that actually knows why he is going to war. Be amused as these mindless hormones taunt innocent, Iraqi women with horrible, vulgar gestures. Let every liberal bone within you be pleased as these same savages will defile Iraqi corpses, stop a football game to have homosexual sex with each other and masturbate as often as they drink water. Learn that every American wife is a prostitute and unfaithful to husbands that go off to war. Yes bring your family!

Anybody with a right mind that is not making a suicide bomb and planning a Jihad would not pay money to see that kind of movie. The producers of the film (and I use the word film in the same way I would describe the yellow layer on my teeth in the morning) knew the previous fact and were smart not to be upfront as to who they are.

The fact is there is not actually any war in this "Gulf war" movie. No scratch that, there are two blink-and-you-missed-it war scenes. One is when the mindless and incompetent American Military kills their own Marines by an A-10 that flies like the pilot is drunk. Then there is the other war scene where we see the aftermath from the savage Americans turning on fleeing and innocent civilians.

There was nothing in the movie about anything real that actually happened in the Gulf war; nothing that we watched live on CNN. Nothing was included about the liberation of Kuwait; nothing about the coalition of multiple nations from all over the world. The entire two hours was just a sick and profane portrayal of senseless American soldiers in a bloodthirsty fraternity of latent homosexuals. I was not impressed.

This movie is vulgar, rude, obscene and offensive to anyone with a conscience and without one redeeming virtue. Oh you will hear that the cinematography is great and yes you will be stunned if you have never seen sand before or pornography or full frontal nudity of lots of guys in a never ending shower shot. Wow!

It offers not a single positive portrayal of a professional Marine or recruit. It slanders the Marines and the Military in general. It makes weak minded people think those that served were idiots. It is designed to rile up that socialist/terrorist part of you and make a stand against anything red, white and blue.

JARHEAD will be a huge hit in Iran, Syria and the Palestinian controlled parts of Israel. Oh, I'm sure it will go over big in Boston, Washington State and the northern part of California too.

I give this movie a thumbs down while pointing my index finger toward the word of God and I say *"Do not be deceived, my beloved brethren."* **(James 1:16)** Jesus said that in the last days men would call good evil and evil good.

Just like Jesus said would one day happen, in this day we literally say something is "bad" meaning it is actually good. This movie is such an example; portraying a righteous cause and the dedicated selflessness of soldiers as something terrible and vulgar. Don't buy it and don't pay for it at the movies.

The American military is still an honorable profession, full of disciplined and moral men and women and if you don't like them you can kiss their military grits!

Semper Fi, in Jesus name.

SOMETHING TO SIP ON:

It was with this column I began to get my "hate mail." One lady even saying that she was going to make it "her personal business" to get in my face when I "least expected it." My letter back to her was that I was not your average Baptist and that I've got plenty of face to go around.

I also apologized for disappointing her for being an American that really loved America, a Christian that really hated filth and a Texan that really was conservative. Who would have ever figured a guy, in this day and age, to be authentic, genuine and what he actually advertises.

I'm sure she thought I should be more 'Seeker Sensitive,' politically correct and full of the liberal hogwash that sells so many books these days.

After all, my column didn't make her feel good or teach her a self help principle nor did I write it with a smile and like I was speaking in Mr. Roger's neighborhood. That's the way America's biggest TV preachers are now, so there is no wonder she was shocked at my column. Bless her heart.

The Brewer doesn't sign up for that mess. Sometimes the cup gets strong.

THE LION, THE WITCH, THE WARDROBE -- AND THE BREWER

My weekends are a lot like a Jesus freak's version of the "Mardi Gras" and on Sunday night I typically go home and promptly fall into a coma. Last Sunday night was different. My boys and I caught the 10:00 pm showing of THE CHRONICALS OF NARNIA. I was glad we did and the conversation we had after the movie was well-worth the $24 unbelievable bucks it cost to get us in.

This week's cup of Jehovah java takes you to the movies for some local flavor and a Christian perspective on The Lion, the Witch and the Wardrobe.

No doubt you have heard the controversies and the hoopla over this flick. People that want it to be the "Lord of the Rings" are mad at how nice the movie is. A lot of C.S. Lewis fans that want it to be more theological are upset that it has such a huge war scene in it. The ACLU is mad because they smell some form of Christianity the way the big nosed dude in Chitty-Chitty-Bang-Bang can sniff out a child.

So what is the Brewer's take and why should any Christian care what's on at the movies? While God has called Christians to be separate, He has never called us to be hermits.

The movies influence this generation the same way the weather used to influence farmers. It's what they talk about; it's what they plan things around and what they constantly allow to mold their thinking. It's an arena that Christians had better be well versed in if they intend on talking a language that this culture can understand.

Movies are often excellent metaphors for spiritual principles and a great way for a Christian to point out what the Bible is saying in a way that is familiar to the hearer. I use scenes in movies all the time to illustrate what the Bible says in black and white. This is a media oriented culture and we ignore that fact at our own peril.

Jesus did the same thing 2000 years ago by using secular events and otherwise nonreligious scenarios that were easily understood by the culture of His day. He used them as illustrations to represent biblical truth and spiritual principles.

He would point to the farmer or to the woman sweeping her house or to the fisherman and say, "The kingdom of heaven is just like that." Those settings were great ways to preach a sermon and many sermons are being preached at our theaters today, but very few by Christians.

For people that hate capitalism and believe America is the devil and all that is evil in the world, they can line up to say "Amen" in movies like "Jarhead" and more recently "Syriana." It's called "agenda film making" and the most famous to deliver its well known leftists political tomes are names like Oliver Stone, Clinton Tarantino and Michael Moore.

It's no exaggeration to claim that there is no such thing as a Pro-Christian, family friendly left winged agenda film. It is not on the map. If it has a liberal or socialist agenda you can also bet big money that it will be wall to wall with filthy language, pointless porno and will go way out of its way to put blood and guts where it isn't needed.

The very rare flip side of that Hollywood coin is a movie like The Chronicles of Narnia. A fantasy film for kids but with an obvious Christian parallel or as the Bible would put it, a parable. In most movies, the Christian symbolism is completely accidental, but because C.S. Lewis wrote it, it's obviously purely intentional.

To me, looking for the symbolism is a fun part of the whole movie going experience. It was a lot like looking for Albert Hitchcock walking through one of his scenes in a little cameo as he so often does in his movies. You spot a Christian metaphor and it's a lot like spotting the point where Arnold says "I'll be back."

For a Bible thumper, it's easy to pick up on some of those and fun to talk about afterwards. For example, Narnia is a lot like Eternity. It's discovered during a game of Hide and Seek.

Ask, and it shall be given you; seek, and ye shall find; knock, and it shall be opened unto you.
Luke 11:9

The door is through the wardrobe or what we westerners would call the closet.

But thou, when thou prayest, enter into thy closet, and when thou hast shut thy door, pray to thy Father which is in secret; and thy Father which seeth in secret shall reward thee openly.
Matthew 6:6

Lucy, the little girl, is the one that makes the discovery of Narnia.

> *And said, Verily I say unto you, except ye be converted,*
> *and become as little children,*
> *ye shall not enter into the kingdom of heaven.*
> **Matthew 18:3**

We could go on and on but from the very beginning of the Narnia adventure it is packed full of biblical symbols that range from the King of Kings being a lion, right down to His triumphant declaration of, "It is finished."

But the thing I really like about this movie is that you don't have to have a clue about the Bible to understand the message of sacrifice. The king Himself is willing to give up his life in order to "save" the life of a traitor.

The most important message the Bible delivers is that Jesus Christ gave His sinless life for us that have sinned. He took on the penalty of eternal death so we would not have to suffer that penalty. The wonderful 'rest of the story' is that because He was sinless, He had the power to conquer death and He slapped hell in the face while He was there.

The Lion, the Witch and the Wardrobe might be just a silly movie but the biblical message it conveys is a truth that needs to be told in every arena possible. It's our job as Christians to connect the dots.

SOMETHING TO SIP ON:

A short Biography of C.S Lewis.

Clive Staples Lewis was born in Belfast, Ireland, to Albert James Lewis and Flora Augusta Hamilton Lewis. As a boy, he adopted the name "Jack" just because he liked the sound of it. From that point on, his friends called him Jack.

Lewis' mother died in 1908, and he was sent to a number of different schools in England. In about 1913, he abandoned his childhood Christian faith and pursued all kinds of education and philosophy.

In 1929, he became a theist: "In the Trinity Term of 1929 I gave in, and admitted that God was God, and knelt and prayed..." Ultimately, in 1931, he returned to Christianity.

Lewis loved to read, and his father's house was filled with books. He would often say that finding a book he hadn't read was as easy as finding a blade of grass.

In 1916 Lewis won a scholarship to Oxford University. However in 1917 he enlisted in the British Army, and was commissioned an officer in the 3rd Battalion, Somerset Light Infantry.

He arrived at the front line in the Somme Valley in France on his 19th birthday. He was wounded during the Battle of Arras, and on his recovery was assigned duty back to England. He was discharged in December 1918, and returned to his studies.

Later Lewis taught as a fellow professor at Oxford for nearly thirty years, from 1925 to 1954. After that he was the first Professor of Medieval and Renaissance Literature at the University of Cambridge.

The Chronicles of Narnia is a series of seven fantasy novels for children; it is by far the most popular of his works. The books were published in an order different from how they take place. In chronological order, the seven books are: The Magician's Nephew, The Lion, the Witch and the Wardrobe, The Horse and His Boy, Prince Caspian, The Voyage of the Dawn Treader, The Silver Chair, and The Last Battle.

People that are into it think that the books should be read in order of publication, beginning with The Lion, the Witch and the Wardrobe (followed by Caspian, Dawn Treader, Silver Chair, Horse, Magician's Nephew and Last Battle).

Lewis died November 22, 1963, at the Oxford home he shared with his brother, Warren. He is buried in the Headington Quarry Churchyard, Oxford, England

Other works include Mere Christianity, The Great Divorce, and The Screw tape Letters.

PEARL HARBOR'S DEFINING MOMENT

There are defining moments for every nation, every generation and in fact every individual. Some of those defining moments might include your high school graduation or depending on your convictions, the first or perhaps the 5th time you got yourself married. Other defining moments might include the birth of a child or the death of a loved one. They are moments that shape a person's life for the rest of their life and mark where things will never be the same again.

In our nation's brief history, we have had many defining moments. One of the greatest being the most recent, a date we will know forever as 9-11. But fifty years before we ever saw the images of those tumbling towers there was another date that for that generation marked a change in the attitude and in the very definition of what it meant to be an American. On Monday morning, every paper in America would call it "a day of infamy."

On December the 7th in 1941, a whole bunch of planes with red circles on their wings flew over the mountains of Hawaii and into a harbor called Pearl. What happened over the next few minutes was unthinkable. America-the good guys, were soundly defeated in every way that could be calculated.

At the end of the day, eight battleships were sunk, the others were damaged, our combat planes were destroyed and over 2400 Americans were no longer with us. In one single carefully-planned and well-executed stroke, the Japanese removed the United State's battleship force as a possible threat to the Empire's southward expansion and policy to make the world Japan's.

An outrage in America followed that silenced Joe Kennedy of Massachusetts and the pacifists of the day. For the next four years it was just flat out seen as un-American to not dedicate your time, talent and treasure, even your life, to conquering the enemy. For a brief time, America was totally united because we truly understood what was at stake and in those days we didn't have 150 channels to divert our attention.

Defining moments will do that to a person or in this case a nation.

The truth of the matter is that in each person's life, there are moments, both positive and negative, which have defined and redefined who we are and how we view the world. We all experience events that are so extreme, they penetrate our conciseness and affect the very core of our lives.

However, there are others, in fact a minority on this planet, that find their lives shaped and defined not only by the events of their day but by the Word that has been spoken into them. These strange people are called Christians and they follow a Savior called Jesus Christ.

For a Christian, there is no greater defining moment then when he came to the understanding he was not God and Jesus Christ is. That day or that hour or that small period of time where he consciously surrendered his life to his relationship with his Lord, is a moment that should redefine him for the rest of his life.

When I was saved back in '86, it was as if an atomic bomb went off. It didn't just affect me, it affected everyone around me. People would drive over to my mom's just to get a look at me, like I had grown a third eye. "Is it true?" folks would ask. "We heard you have become a Jesus freak." "It's much worse than you think." I would reply.

The reason for all the fuss is because there was an immediate and stark contrast in what I was before Christ entered my life, from the person I became after I was saved. For me, meeting the person of Jesus Christ was truly a defining moment. From that moment on, my behavior, my actions, my friends, my thoughts, my goals, my speech, my habits and literally everything about me was defined by my relationship with Christ and by the Word of God.

My History is split down the middle the same way that Human history is, B.C and A.D. I don't even look the same. People would ask me, "Troy, have you lost weight?" I would say "Just the weight of the world." Since then, I have progressed and grown and my walk as a Christian has redefined me over and over again as I grow in revelation and faith.

I wonder about so-called Christians that never have a defining moment. I don't really get it when someone says that they have been "saved" yet their life doesn't change at all. It worries me to see people signing up to join big churches but not sighing up to dedicate their lives to Christ.

The typical "Cultural Christian" sees Jesus as a "quick fix" or "self help" and not as the King He really is. It is those very same people who later complain, God has failed them somehow, when in fact they never knew Him at all.

I believe it is impossible to have a true encounter with Christ that does not change your life. This might just sound like words but it is as real as the black on the white pages you are reading.

Jesus said you can tell what a tree is by the fruit it bears. The mark of a true Christian has nothing to do with church membership or financial contribution or what popular books you are reading. You can tell when it's the "real deal" because the change in that person's life is the "real deal."

Sixty four years ago, the attack on Pearl Harbor completely redefined America as anyone had known her. Instead of cowering in our darkest hour we rose up like an awakened giant and nothing was the same after that. Just like that, a true personal encounter with Christ should and does promise to change who you are in every way a person can be changed.

SOMETHING TO SIP ON:

My daughter Meagan helped me write this column. She was home on a weekend leave from her studies at the Honor Academy, Teen Mania's Bible College.

She is an amazing young woman. She's beautiful and smart. She loves to travel and be involved with people. She has a very tender heart and incredibly giving spirit. People love her and she loves her daddy. I am so proud of her.

I don't think there is any higher accolade I could say about Meagan than she loves Jesus with all her heart and she is committed to her walk in Christ.

When I see Meagan I see an answered prayer.

I have no greater joy than to hear that my children walk in truth.
3 John 1:4

TIS THE SEASON TO BE OFFENDED

While people check their cringe meters and political correctness handbooks to see if they should say happy Chanukah, Ramadan, Quanza or Winter Solstice, most are selling out for the happy holiday thing. The Brewer sips his coffee, shakes his head and says in his really cool Texas accent, "Yeppers, America's goin' to hell!"

Not to worry – you liberal progressives. People have been well programmed to make a quick ethnic assessment of others and after referring to their brainwashed holiday profile, will continue to spread whatever cheer they deem appropriate.

It amazes me that everyone is so worried about connecting people with Christ at Christmas time. It's like the new unspoken policy is to be respectful of every religious figure except for Jesus and respect all people groups except of course for Christians; tis' the season to throw Jesus out the window.

The main reason for this is because the American church is full of a bunch of seeker friendly, limp wristed, television hosts instead of true spiritual leaders. Why should the world be afraid to dis Christians? What are we going to do?

When a Christian leader does stand up against the hijacking of American culture, he brings on a firestorm of criticism that few are willing to stomach. A good example of this is Dr. James Dobson's recent stand to pull Focus on the Family out of the Wells Fargo banking system.

This last year, a Gay Pride Festival event in San Francisco, called 'Leather Alley," was hosted and staged in the parking lot of a Wells Fargo bank. Leather Alley is one of the most wicked and perverse events that happens in the United States. After that, Focus on the Family learned that it was posted on Fargo's Web site that the bank has donated more than $14 million to homosexual organizations.

In response to Focus on the Family, the bank says "we direct our giving to areas that we believe are important to the future of our nation's vitality and success: community development, education and human services."

When I read that, I nearly dropped my cup! Wells Fargo bank has gone on the record by stating it thinks it is important to our nation's success that leather-clad homosexuals parade in decadence through their parking lots.

I wonder where these people were educated. What part of human history are they basing their evaluation of a nation's success? In their environmentally friendly, smoke free executive room in San Francisco, they not only agree to it but support it to the tune of $14,000,000.00!

That money did not feed a single hungry American or educate one single child but it sure bought a lot of leather at Bruce's Whip Emporium. Way to make a difference guys!

These are the same types of executives that worry about offending people by saying the dreaded C-word. How crazy is that?

In the messed minds of Wells Fargo executives their policy is reasonable. You and your family may have to endure men dressed in leather bikinis dancing to the tune of "YMCA" but don't let that stop you from cashing your check. They have fixed it so you will never endure a nativity scene or the vulgar gesture of hearing the words "Merry Christmas." Thank you for your concern and responsible protection of my family's feelings.

Wells Fargo executives, it is the Brewer's humble opinion that you are smoking crack and need to wake up out of your politically correct coma.

So what's the big deal, you might ask, about Christmas and why should we care if other religions try to steal the spotlight at this time of year. Once more, why should we care if a corporate giant tries to move Christmas into some generic holiday?

Like Ricky said to Lucy fifty years ago, "Let me 'splain."

2000 before Ricky and Lucy, when the angel Gabriel announced the birth of the promised Messiah, a young Lady named Mary asked an important Question, "How can these things be?"

The reply was recorded in **Luke 1:37**, *"With God all things shall be possible."*

See, to a Christian, that's what the birth of Jesus is all about. It's about the realization that with God all things are possible and it doesn't matter how off the wall His promises are. God is a God that can be trusted because He will keep his promises and this was proven first at the birth of Jesus Christ. Christmas is The Promise fulfilled.

For 4000 years God promised He would send a messiah. His descriptions trickled out of prophecies throughout the centuries. He would be a deliverer, a fixer of the problem, a savior, a heroic rescuer, an emancipator and even a ransom for many.

As the centuries rolled by and men began to see how pitifully far from God we were, it also became apparent that this kind of person had never existed. Because what was needed was a God, that was a man; a living oxymoron. A compassionate destroyer that had all power was above all and yet humble and willing to lay down everything.

So when men would study and see what it would take in order for us to be saved, they would inevitably come to the conclusion that it was just too impossible. Yet God continued promising.

He wrote it in the heavens, He penned it in his book He shouted it through his prophets and He didn't care how impossible it was. He just said, "I promise." The more God promised the more confusing it would be to people who studied the promise and the greater the impossibility appeared.

There were at least 72 very specific prophesies or promises written in scripture about this Messiah. To the reader, they all seemed to contradict each other and the promises God made about the appearance of His son, were impossible to fulfill. Yet Jesus showed up and made it all make sense. That's what He did at His birth and that is what He still does today. That's what we celebrate at Christmas.

There is no hope in saying "happy holidays" but there is hope in saying "Merry Christmas."

So from The Brewer and the folks at Open Door Ministries let me cut through the red tape with the Joy that can only be found in Christ Jesus.

MERRY CHRISTMAS, JOSHUA!!

SOMETHING TO SIP ON:

Several biblical prophecies on the offense and persecution of the last days:

Matthew 10:21-22
"Now brother will deliver up brother to death, and a father his child; and children will rise up against parents and cause them to be put to death. And you will be hated by all for My name's sake."

Matthew 24:8-14
"... you will be hated by all nations for My name's sake... And then many will be offended, will betray one another, and will hate one another. Then many false prophets will rise up and deceive many. And because lawlessness will abound, the love of many will grow cold. But he who endures to the end shall be saved."

Mark 13:11-13
"Now brother will betray brother to death, and a father his child; and children will rise up against parents and cause them to be put to death. And you will be hated by all for My name's sake. But he who endures to the end shall be saved."

2 Timothy 3:1-5, 10-14
"But know this, that in the last days perilous times will come: For men will be lovers of themselves, lovers of money, boasters, proud, blasphemers, disobedient to parents,

unthankful, unholy, unloving, unforgiving, slanderers, without self-control, brutal, despisers of good, traitors, headstrong, haughty, lovers of pleasure rather than lovers of God.... And from such people turn away!

"...all who desire to live godly in Christ Jesus will suffer persecution. But evil men and impostors will grow worse and worse, deceiving and being deceived. But you must continue in the things which you have learned"

Luke 21:12-16

"...they will lay hands on you and persecute you. They will deliver you to synagogues and prisons, and you will be brought before kings and governors, and all on account of my name. This will result in your being witnesses to them. But make up your mind not to worry beforehand how you will defend yourselves. For I will give you words and wisdom that none of your adversaries will be able to resist or contradict. You will be betrayed even by parents, brothers, relatives and friends, and they will put some of you to death."

Revelation 17:6

"I saw the woman, drunk with the blood of the saints and with the blood of the martyrs of Jesus. And when I saw her, I marveled with great amazement."

THE GIFT THAT GAVE EVERYTHING

Hello, Johnson County. This column represents the bottom of the pot for this year's "FRESH FROM THE BREWER." It's the last column for this year and there is just enough left for one last sip from the Carpenter's Cup.

Our mission's trip to the border last week was an outstanding example of how you can see God's love at Christmas time. A big team from Open Door Ministries took 1,000 boxes of toys and several pallets of goodies south to Brownsville, Texas/ Matamoras, Mexico for a children's outreach.

The sights and sounds of border towns are just plain different than the norm of anywhere else. Though it is not new to me, it is still somewhat of a sensory overload. At the end of the day you lay there staring at the ceiling of your hotel room trying to sort through everything in your head the way you file pictures in a scrapbook. There are just so many scenes and conversations to go through.

I love the frontier. Borders represent physical, emotional, national and even spiritual places where lines are drawn and things are done differently. It is a place where miracles can happen.

This was my 32nd mission trip to Mexico and every time I go, I see something brand new. I see the kind of things you would expect to see -- such as extreme poverty, street vendors, tons of pharmacies and lots of kids, but because of the nature of our trips, we get to see things that very few ever do.

It's funny how a sight, a sound or a smell will trigger your memory and jolt your attention onto something that you otherwise would have forgotten.

I remember 8 years ago, a little boy by the name of Arturo that was filling milk jugs with water to take back home. He had stood in line all night to get his chance at the single water spigot for a community of thousands. At the time I met him, he had just begun to trickle brown water into his containers.

My brother-in-law, Daniel Meyer, asked him if he would take twenty dollars for those ten gallons of brown Mexican water. Arturo said no and continued holding his milk jug under the dirty trickle. "What about $30?" he asked and Arturo never flinched.

"I'll give you $50 for that water, right now," Daniel offered. Still no deal and when he was finished, that little boy loaded up his gallons and began heading back to his family.

You see, Daniel and I both understood how important that water was to Arturo. It might not have been much, but it was all he had. There was no way any gringo was going to talk him out of it. He was committed to something that most others would quickly reject, because it was precious to him.

Though I never saw him again, Arturo has preached to me several times through the years. I thought a lot about him as we handed out toys to thousands of kids down there last week. I kept finding myself looking for him but of course he's not a little boy any more. He was around twelve then and that would make him around twenty now.

Through a haze in the hopeful part of my mind, I vision that today Arturo lives a completely different life. No longer living in the trash dumps where he grew up, he somehow is successful and has a family of his own. My little dream says that he comes home to a beautiful young wife that is proud of him and he already has a child that will never know what it is like to suffer through the pains of true poverty.

I don't know what the reality of Arturo's life is or even if he is alive at all today. I do know this, I learned more about my walk with Jesus though him than most would learn through seminary. Though the jugs of brown water didn't look like much to others, what he had was precious to him and he was completely committed and faithful to hanging onto it.

My hope in Jesus Christ may not look like much to others but it is so precious to me. My relationship with the Lord may be rejected by most but I won't let anybody talk me out of it. There are many readers today that feel the same way and I encourage you this Christmas.

I hope that you can take the gifts in life God has trusted to you and hold them close because they really are precious to you. I hope more than anything that you will accept the greatest gift that has ever been offered to anyone.

You may of heard that "God so loved the word He gave His only begotten Son," as John 3:16 says but consider the fact that people have loved themselves so much they have never bothered to receive that "unspeakable gift" (2 Corinthians 9:15) offered to them.

2000 years ago Jesus met somebody at the water well in her neighborhood. In the same way, He encouraged her to open God's present for her life.

Jesus answered and said to her, If thou knewest the gift of God, and who it is that saith to thee, Give me to drink; thou wouldst have asked him, and he would have given thee living water.
John 4:10

You've heard of the gift that keeps on giving. Jesus is the gift that returned to give everything.

Unwrap your presents, kids and don't forget to say a prayer for Arturo.

SOMETHING TO SIP ON:

James 1:17
Every good gift and every perfect gift is from above, and cometh down from the Father of lights, with whom is no variableness, neither shadow of turning.

"Every good gift" refers to things that are not evil or things that are Holy and every perfect gift refers to things that are complete and glorify God. Those really are precious gifts.

His thoughts towards you are good as the Bible says. Anytime you see things that are good you see things that have to do with the natural realm. That's why at the end of every day in the creation story God said that it was Good.

So all the gifts He has given you in the natural are "good." Food and drink, physical comfort, good music, the gratification of hard work, the smell of fresh air, even the wonder of approaching storms; these are all good gifts from your Father.

All of the gifts He has given you in the Spiritual are "perfect." How precious are those spiritual gifts and how essential, even more so than our natural gifts?

Notice it says that that there is neither variance nor shadow of turning in our "father of lights." This is a reference to some days being brighter than others and James wants you to know God has "Sunny Day" gifts for you every day of the year.

Be sure you unwrap your "Sunny Day" gift today.

THE LAST WORD

In this week's confessions of a highly caffeinated Christian, I bring you the last sip of Fresh from the Brewer. It's the last column for the Joshua Star in 2005 and it is my privilege to share this cup with you.

Being the self professed weirdo that I am, I tend to pay attention to otherwise strange things. About ten years ago I started collecting the last words of famous fictional characters and paying attention to the last things said in my favorite movies and books

Here are some examples of a few you might recognize.
A River Runs Through It: "I am haunted by waters."
Tombstone: "Tom Mix wept."
John Wayne in True Grit: "Come and visit a fat old man sometime."
Captain Ahab in Moby Dick: "Thus, I give up the spear!"
Captain James Tiberius Kirk of Star Trek Generations: "Well it was fun, oh my."

Then there are famous last words of real people; a very odd but delightful field of study in its very nature consists of nothing but conclusions.

Despite the basic *graveness*, pardon the pun, of the situation that individual's face at the moment of their death, there have been those that sprang a joke and some of them really good ones.

King Louis the 14th told his wife he regretted leaving her, but at her age he expected to see her shortly again. Then he died before she could slap him.

William Palmer, a man convicted in 1920 of poisoning his friend was silent when they put the noose around his neck. The hangman instructed him to step up onto the trap door and Palmer asked, "Are you sure it's safe?"

James Rodgers, a convicted murderer executed in 1960 in Nevada, was asked by the rifle squad commander if he had any last request. "Why yes...a bullet proof vest, please!"

Oscar Wilde the famous writer, died November 30, 1900 saying, "Either that wallpaper goes, or I do."

W.C. Fields, after falling to the floor and in terrible pain, calmed down, looked at the person trying to help him and said, "On the whole, I'd rather be in Philadelphia."

Douglass Fairbanks died in 1939. When he fell down someone asked him if he was okay. "I never felt better," he said with his last breath.

Georges Jacques Danton, a French radical, became the acknowledged leader of the revolution following the storming of the Bastille in 1789. Eventually 'out-radicaled' by someone else, he was sentenced to death. Asked to formally reply to the revolutionary tribunal that sentenced him, he defiantly began, "My address will soon be annihilation. As for my name, you will find it in the pantheon of history." Later as he placed his neck in the guillotine, he gave the executioner his final instructions. "Show my head to the people. It really is worth seeing."

One of my all time favorites are the last words of Wilson Mizner who died in 1933. Wilson Mizner was a U.S. writer, gambler and someone who put his trust in Jesus Christ at the very end of his life. On his deathbed, just before dying, he briefly regained consciousness and found a priest standing over him. Mizner waved the priest away saying, "Why should I talk to you? I've just been talking to your boss."

Many times the words that a Christian speaks as he faces eternity are a wonderful testimony.

Solomon Foot, the senator and Master of Parliamentary Law, died in his bed in 1866 with these last words. "What? Can this be death, has it come already? I see it, I see it! The gates are wide open it's beautiful! It's beautiful!"

John Lambert, the protestant Christian martyr burned in Smithfield England in 1538 held up his burning hands and cried "None but Christ, none but Christ!"

William Tyndale, the famous reformer and martyr has an awesome testimony. Because the King of England hated Tyndale so much for daring to defy the church and print the Bible in a common language for common people, he sent a scribe to write down his last words. The idea was to frame and hang the word, for all to read the King's enemies' dying plea for mercy. Mere seconds before dying, Tyndale cried out with his last breath these words for the scribe to record, "Lord, open the King of England's eyes!"

Robert Bruce, the King of Scotland who lived from 1274 to 1329 said, "Now, God be with you, my dear children. I have breakfasted with you and shall sup with my Lord Jesus Christ."

A lady named Edith Cavell was the Senior Matron of a British Red Cross Hospital stationed in Brussels during the first months of World War I. After the German Army overran neutral Belgium, Cavell and a team of nurses secretly treated hundreds of allied soldiers. When the soldiers were well enough to travel, Cavell provided them with civilian clothes, false identification, money, and an escort to the border.

In August, 1915, she was arrested, court-martialed for spying, and sentenced to death; she was shot by a German firing squad the following October. "I expected my sentence and believe it was just. Standing, as I do, in the view of God and eternity I realize that patriotism is not enough. I must have no hatred or bitterness to anyone."

Martin Luther died on February 17, 1546 at the age of 63. After he said his goodbyes to his family and friends, he asked they all remain quiet and in prayer with him for the last few minutes of his life. He then said, "I commend my Spirit into thy hands, thou hast redeemed me, oh God of Truth!" Then he slowly recited the words of John 3:16 over and over until he died.

There are a lot of different ways we could end the last word for this year. But let me do so the same way the Bible ends. There are 31,175 verses in the old King James and the very last verse is a great word and the Brewer's prayer for you and yours.

The grace of our Lord Jesus Christ be with you all. Amen.
Revelation 22:21

SOMETHING TO SIP ON:

Take a good look at the very last words of the Old Testament and compare them with the very last words of the New Testament.

The Old Testament ends in Malachi with "....I will smite the earth with a curse." The very last word of the Old Testament under the old covenant is the word "Curse."

If you fast forward to the end of the New Testament you find a blessing. You can see by the last word of both books that we have moved from the threat of a curse to the promise of a blessing and guess who has entered into the picture? Jesus! That's what happens every time Jesus enters into any picture.

GOOD TO THE LAST DROP
The Closing Thank You

In closing I have to go back to the beginning for without Dale Gosser and Lowell Brown of the Cleburne Times review giving me a chance, there would not be a *"Fresh from the Brewer"* column today.

They made my column available to the good people of Johnson County, Texas and as they say, the rest is history!

I want to also say that I highly appreciate Daun Eierdam, Managing Editor of the Joshua Star newspaper.

Daun was the driving force behind the creation of the opinions page in the Star which became home to the *"Fresh from the Brewer"* articles.

Daun's insight, professionalism and attention to detail have helped shape the way *"Fresh from the Brewer"* looks today.

His numerous and helpful tidbits of wisdom have jazzed up the column and made it look the way a newspaper column should look. He also made me look smarter than a feller from Johnson County has a right to.

Thank you Ike Massey for publishing the star group papers the way you do and for allowing me to be in your papers.

Thank you to The North Texas e-news and particularly Allen Rich for running the columns.

Thank you to Penny Maguire and Susan Walker from the Leakey Star. I love having a column in the Hill country,

Thank you Tom Beasley at the Crowley Star for the really cool picture and for putting up with me.

Thank you to John Moseley and Susanne Reed of The Big Spring Harold. Your paper is an oasis in the west Texas desert.

I also say a big thank you to Carol Bianchi, you are a blessing to me and to everyone that reads this book. Your proof reading continues to change my chicken pecks into something fairly legible.

I thank you and Chuck both for being the people that you are and for being a friend to this ministry. You both are a big blessing

A great Big Thank you also goes to Steve Ashley for your help and general support you give me in so much that happened with FFTB.

Finally, a great big thank you goes out to the people who have supported our ministry this year and made this book possible.

I thank God for my wife and my kids. I love you so much and I am so proud of all of you.

Blessings and Peace on "all ya'll."

ONE MORE THING TO SIP ON:

Jesus asks, *Are ye able to drink of the cup that I shall drink of, and to be baptized with the baptism that I am baptized with?* **Matt 20:22**

The Brewer asks, "Will you????"

ABOUT THE AUTHOR

Troy Brewer drinks coffee, diets often and loves Jesus in Johnson County, Texas. A life long resident of the Joshua area, his church continues to love him in spite of what he did there before he was saved.

He and his wife Leanna pastor Open Door Ministries, an outreach church that gives away over a million pounds of food and goods every year to poor families and struggling people. They also head up Answer International, a mission ministry and S.P.A.R.K International, (Serving, Protecting and Raising Kids) an outreach that builds and supports orphanages throughout the world.

His music has reached untold numbers throughout the world and to date he has 6 CD's to his credit.

Troy is also the author of "Miracles with A Message", "Soul Invasion" and "Fresh from the Brewer" the first volume.

He is also a noted draw-er of musclemen and cars with 50 engines. He has 4 kids, Maegan, Benjamin, Luke and Rhema. They generally get along, even on mornings before he has his first cup.

He can be contacted at:
P.O. Box 1349   Joshua, TX 76058
817-297-6911
www.opendoorministries.org

Please let us know if this book has blessed you and if not, please disregard all contact information.

Printed in the United States
67207LVS00002B/343-405